VOLUME II 1968-1974

Sarah Sink Eames

COLLECTOR BOOKS
A Division of Schroeder Publishing Co., Inc.

The current values of this book should be used only as a guide. They are not intended to set prices, which vary from one section of the country to another. Auction prices as well as dealer prices vary greatly and are affected by condition as well as demand. Neither the Author nor the Publisher nor Mattel, Inc. assumes responsibility for any losses that might be incurred as a result of consulting this guide.

Searching for a Publisher?

We are always looking for knowledgeable people considered to be experts within their fields. If you feel that there is a real need for a book on your collectible subject and have a large comprehensive collection, contact Collector Books.

Cover Design: Beth Summers
Book Design: Donna Ballard

On the Cover:

Talking Barbie doll #1115 is wearing Sparkle Squares #1814 (1968 – 1969).
For more information on outfit, see page 9.

Contents

Dedication

This book is dedicated to my mother, Printice Phillips Sink, who was a great Barbie doll playmate!

Acknowledgments

Many thanks are due to a host of people who have in some way or ways made this book possible. Here are just a few!

Marlene Anderson, Joan Ashabraner, Susan Baldock, Hande Ballweg, Shirley Berry, Evelyn Blake, Peggy Bowling, Marjorie Buxton, Beulah Caswell, Laura Choquette, Marie Cluster, Irena Creaser, Ruth Cronk, Pat Derelanko, Steffi Deutsch, Sibyl DeWein, Alan and Joy Eadline, Alice Gallagher, Gloria Greenstreet, Sandra Goss, Ellie Haynes, Joann Hemminger, Phyllis Houston, Ruth Jacobson, Helmut Jahn, Dieter Jeschke, Janice Kaderly, Georgia Kromer, Shirley Larsen, Bernice Lelito, Franklin Lim Liao, Jenny Litos, A. Glenn Mandeville, Susan Manos, Dori O'Melia, Grace Otto, Robin Reynolds, Michael Sanchez, Virginia Slade, Carol Spencer, Ingelore Streng, George and Florence Theriault, Carole Triplett, Connie Toth, Diane and Beth Wright.

Introduction

This book contains the continuation of documentation of the wardrobes of the Barbie doll, her family and friends. Volume I featured the beginning years of 1959 through 1967. In Volume II, we progress from 1968 through 1974 which is another exciting time period to study. The quality, detail, and accessorization of the costumes continued through the early 1970s. And, although in some cases expenses were cut in the Best Buy outfits, there is still that Barbie doll flair and interest. I could not collect only the earliest outfits without the rest of the story! Barbie doll's world continues to tell, through her lifestyle, the story of who we are. This is shown in our fashion choices which depict our lifestyle and Barbie doll is a mirror image of that lifestyle—in miniature!

As with Volume I, the book is broken into chapters which contain the outfits for each of the dolls for that particular year. The year's content is based on Mattel's dealer catalogs for dating. The costumes are photographed out of the box wherever possible to show more detail. This enables the collector to recognize the individual pieces that make up a complete ensemble.

Countries other than Japan, such as Mexico, Korea, Hong Kong, and Taiwan, were sources of the clothing in these later years. 1972 was the last year that the woven clothing labels for Barbie doll and family were used.

Preservation is an issue on the mind of every collector. One reminder concerning the outfits of this era is beware of transparent tape! It was used in some of the packages to hold an outfit in place. As it ages, the adhesive can stain the attached garment. The debate becomes more complicated concerning keeping our collection NRFB or removing items from the package when we are faced with such a deterioration problem.

Finally, don't be reluctant to venture into this era of collecting. There is so much fun and fashion to enjoy from 1968 through 1974. Don't miss the rare pieces and the challenges during these years because they are aesthetically pleasing, collectible, and as much fun as the ones you adored in Volume I.

Chapter I – 1968

World of Barbie Doll

The year featured exciting ideas in the Barbie doll line. Although Ken doll was on a temporary hiatus and no male doll existed in the line, Barbie doll still had great date ensembles and a beautiful new wedding gown!

After the dramatic change in Barbie doll's face mold in 1967, you would think that year could not be topped. However, the wonderful talking dolls were born and this line introduced two new friends, Stacey and Christie dolls.

Barbie doll's wardrobe took a favorite turn. After a trendy (but a bit reserved in some cases) collection of ensembles during the past two years, Barbie doll's wardrobe gave way to full-blown mod styling! The colors were electric, the patterns bold, hem lengths soared above the knee, and the names of the outfits reflected the wild styling! Zokko! Snap-dash! Swirly-cue! Snug-fuzz! Now Wow! Wild 'n Wonderful! Smasheroo! What a fabulous year!

Twenty-four new outfits (16 in spring and eight in fall) were fashioned for Barbie doll with repeats of the 14 most mod outfits from 1967. These repeats were Bouncy Flouncy # 1805, Pajama-Pow! #1806, Disco Dater #1807, Drizzle Dash #1808, Mini Prints #1809, Bermuda Holidays #1810, Tropicana #1460, Sunflower #1683, Underprints #1685, Print A Plenty #1686, Intrigue #1470, Fashion Shiner #1691, Patio Party #1692, and Pink Moonbeams #1694.

Francie doll had a new wardrobe featuring 12 new styles with the repeat of only four from 1967. These repeats were Slumber Number #1271, Hi-Teen #1272, Side-Kick #1273, and Iced Blue #1274. Twiggy doll had four outfits all her own.

The small-fry had great new ensembles as well. Little Tutti and Chris dolls had four new outfits and Skipper doll had eight bright new fashions.

Barbie and Francie dolls had new Fashion Pak assortments added to their wardrobes, too.

Talking Barbie Doll
Original Outfit (1968 – 1969)
#1115

Her original swimsuit featured pink vinyl panties with pink knit top with yellow and pink braid. $25.00

Talking Stacey Doll
Original Outfit (1968 – 1969)
#1125

Cool color waves decorated the knit two-piece suit. A single golden bead button on the shoulder fastened the top. $25.00

Talking Christie Doll
Original Outfit (1968 – 1969)
#1126

Her rose vinyl panties were topped by a green top with pink and green braid. It was made from the same pattern as Talking Barbie doll's suit #1115. $25.00

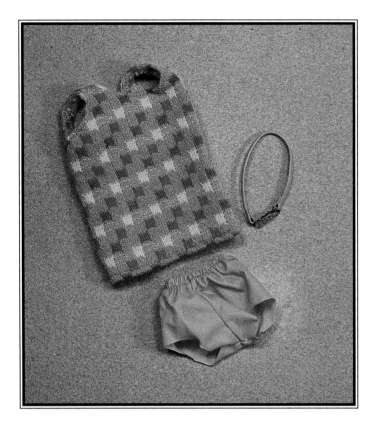

Twist 'n Turn Barbie Doll
Original Outfit (1968)
#1160

Pink knit top with woven print, chartreuse vinyl belt with golden buckle, pink vinyl panties. $35.00

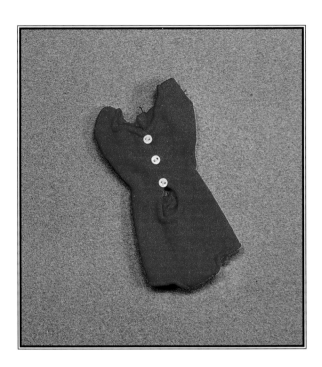

Twist 'n Turn
Stacey Doll
Original Outfit (1968)
#1165

One-piece red Helanca suit with two-piece look in back and cutout in front. Two white buttons accented the front. The color varied from deep red to almost red orange. $35.00

Knit Hit (1968 – 1969)
#1804

Pastel pretty blue and pink soft knit sleeveless sheath with stitching accent on bodice, made a hit wherever Barbie doll went! Blue closed toe pumps accessorized her dress which was found in both lined and unlined versions. $75.00

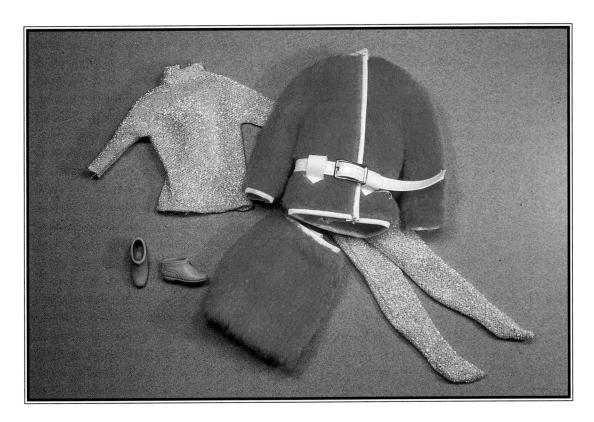

Snug Fuzz (1968 – 1969)
#1813

Barbie doll proved that the suit did not have to be dull! Hot pink plush formed a sheath skirt and the elongated jacket with white vinyl piping at the neck, placket, hem, and sleeves. A low slung white vinyl belt was attached to the jacket with vinyl loops. The outfit was jazzed up even more with a metallic silvertone knit long-sleeved knit top and matching hose. Gray plastic go-go boots completed the wild suit idea. $250.00

Sparkle Squares (1968 – 1969)
#1814

A glamorous evening ensemble fashioned from a beautiful oversize check in a gorgeous lamé. A sleeveless dress fell straight to a gathered white organdy overskirt. A metallic silvertone wide belt defined the dropped waist. Silvertone straps accented the shoulders. The beautifully constructed matching coat featured a full, white organdy lining with ruffle down the front and "diamond" buttons. White glittery hose and white bow shoes completed the outfit Barbie doll chose for elegant evenings on the town. $300.00

Zokko! (1968 – 1969)
#1820

Ready for a night at the disco, Barbie doll wore a soft metallic knit dress with silver sleeveless bodice and blue gathered mini skirt. A silver metallic belt with orange stripe accented the dropped waistline. Orange molded boots were painted metallic silver except for the cuff. Orange plastic drop rectangular earrings completed the space age ensemble! (The earrings were the same design as the ones with Print A Plenty #1686 which were pink.) $150.00

Underliners (1968 – 1969)
#1821

Under fashions at their mod best! A pretty chartreuse, fuchsia, yellow, and turquoise floral print tricot formed the chemise with generous hot pink lace froth at the bust and hem. Hot pink ribbon straps on the chemise matched the hot pink garters on Barbie doll's garter belt. Hose and hot pink open toe shoes completed the set. $150.00

Swirly Cue (1968 – 1969)
#1822

The pretty A-line dress was jazzed up with a racy fabric and a flirty ruffled hem! Swirls and swirls of bright greens, pinks, and blues danced on Barbie doll's sleeveless dress. Geometric earrings featuring a pink rectangle and a chartreuse triangle, plus hot pink closed toe pumps completed Barbie doll's ensemble. $150.00

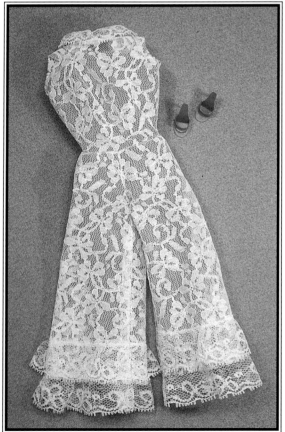

Jump Into Lace (1968)
#1823

Feminine hostess pajamas fit for the perfect hostess—Barbie doll. The white all-over lace design featured a ruffle at the neck and two at the hem. The outfit was lined in a hot pink taffeta and featured matching open toe pumps as accents. $200.00

Snap Dash (1968)
#1824

Yippee! What a way-out look for our cowgirl—Barbie doll! The chartreuse textured dress featured yellow shiny vinyl trim at the collar, placket and cuffs. The collar buttoned down with golden bead buttons. The fashionable accessories were yellow knit knee socks and yellow bow shoes. Topping off the ensemble was Barbie doll's chartreuse felt cowgirl hat with yellow vinyl hat band and ties with a chartreuse slide fastener. $200.00

Night Clouds (1968)
#1841

Barbie doll floated off to dreamland in a mod ruffled gown of yellow, orange, and pink. A pink ribbon rosette accented the bodice and narrow ribbon followed the empire waistline. The sheer yellow peignoir was also mini length and featured two pink ribbon rosettes at the neckline as well as ruffle trim and ribbon ties. $200.00

Togetherness (1968)
#1842

All three components of this "little girl" look combined simply, but artistically together for an innocent impression. The knit fabric featured sweet pink flower stripes which alternate directions, and baby blue solid bands. The sleeveless dress featured a dropped waist bodice using the stripes horizontally. The skirt, on the contrary, used the stripes vertically and the the matching hose went back to the horizontal! The cute bonnet had hot pink ties and a pair of hot pink bow shoes completed Barbie doll's charming look. $200.00

Dancing Stripes (1968)
#1843

This smashing evening outfit featured metallic accents on satin in shades of pink, rose, purple, and palest pink. The coat was lined with pale pink nylon. The sheath dress featured golden straps and double hot pink lace ruffles at the hem. Hot pink closed toe pumps completed Barbie doll's party outfit. $300.00

Extravaganza (1968)
#1844

A spectacular evening gown was fit for the most elegant occasion. A pink tulle cage with glitter dots plunged to the rows of silver braid and fabric flowers with green "leaf" trim at the hem. The halter neckline was formed by a hot pink ruffle on silver braid. The dress had a full lining of hot pink nylon. A silver tone clutch bag, long hot pink gloves, and clear open toe shoes with silvery glitter completed the dramatic ensemble. $350.00

Scene Stealers (1968)
#1845

This fabulous three-piece set featured a pink sheer coat with stand-up collar, placket, and cuffs of satin, a green lamé top with pink satin trim and a three tiered mini skirt with green edging on pink ruffles and satin lining. Hot pink closed toe pumps completed the ensemble. $250.00

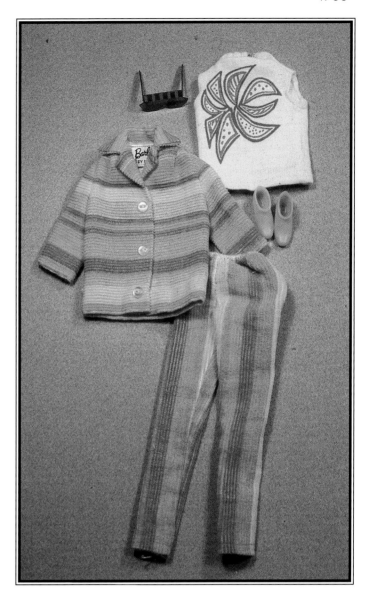

Trailblazers (1968)
#1846

Corduroy was made exciting with narrow and wide bands of orange, chartreuse, pink, and olive. The slacks were topped by a matching jacket with big buttons and a pale yellow tee shirt with a tropical graphic printed on front. Chartreuse go-go boots and green mod plastic glasses with pink vertical stripes completed Barbie doll's fun for the outdoors look. $250.00

All That Jazz (1968 – 1969)
#1848

Another perfect coat and dress ensemble for those elegant evening dinners or parties featured a beautiful, silky play of orange, hot pink, chartreuse, and metallic goldtone stripes. The dress featured a sleeveless bodice and a knife-pleated skirt falling from the dropped waist. The matching coat featured a full lining of chartreuse nylon. A goldtone metallic belt with yellow plastic slide fastener accented the dropped waist on the coat. Sparkle hose and hot pink bow shoes completed the ensemble that looks great on a Twist 'n Turn Barbie with the original orange bow in her hair! $300.00

Wedding Wonder (1968 – 1969)
#1849

Barbie doll modelled this beautifully updated wedding gown. The silhouette took quite a change in direction from the fitted styles of previous years to a full flowing tent that fell gracefully from the shoulders. The fabric was a dotted swiss nylon with a satin stand-up collar that plunged in the back. The hem was accented with white ribbon edging and bows. The dress was fully lined with white satin. The tulle veil was caught into a gathered hat made of the dotted swiss. A bouquet of two white velvet flowers, three buds, and a base of the dotted swiss with a satin ribbon bow and long streamers and white closed toe pumps completed the gracefully modern wedding ensemble. $400.00

Now Wow! (1968 – 1969)
#1853

Wow is right! Barbie doll stepped out in style in a pretty powder blue mini wale corduroy long-sleeved dress. Chartreuse yarn braid formed the scalloped hem border on the sleeves and the yarn ran up the front with a cute bow on the bodice. Her matching corduroy bonnet was timmed with the yarn also. Pale blue hose and blue boots had painted chartreuse trim on the top and tassle front. (These boots were made from the same mold used for Barbie doll's Drum Majorette #0875 outfit from 1964 – 1965.) $200.00

Twinkle Togs (1968 – 1969)
#1854

The perfect little mini dance dress featured a bright turquoise metallic knit top and a chartreuse lined sheer full skirt. This overskirt featured brightly colored metallic horizontal stripes. Sparkly chartreuse hose and turquoise closed toe pumps completed the ensemble. $150.00

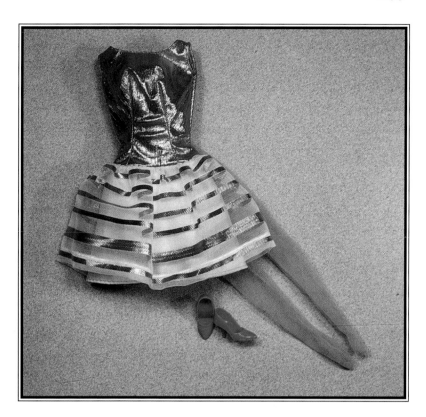

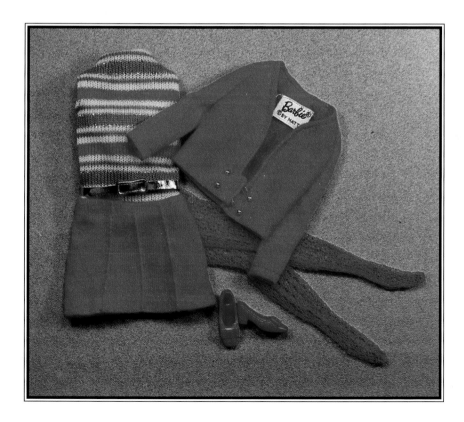

Team Ups (1968 – 1969)
#1855

Fuchsia fashion-a-go-go! The double breasted knit jacket featured four gold-tone bead buttons and long sleeves. It topped a dress with a horizontal striped bodice of green, yellow, fuchsia, and gold with a fuchsia flared skirt. Hot pink closed toe pumps completed the look. $150.00

Wild 'n Wonderful (1968 – 1969)
#1856

This fabulous mini outfit took Barbie doll everywhere in trendy style! The op-art fabric featured geometrics in electric orange, hot pink, green, turquoise, and chartreuse. The fitted sleeveless blouse featured three golden bead buttons and a stand-up collar. The mini skirt had an orange elastic waistband, a tiny patch pocket and featured button detailing. Barbie doll's great knee high sandals were fashioned from orange plastic with cut-outs and golden button closures. Orange plastic panties were also included. An absolutely wonderful look! $200.00

Dreamy Pink (1968 – 1969)
#1857

It is a wonder Barbie doll could sleep in this electric pink gown and peignoir set! Both pieces were fashioned from a hot pink nylon with a sprinkling of dots. The gown was lined in tricot and had hot pink lace straps. The robe featured a frothy flower-trimmed double ruffle at the neck and cuffs. Barbie doll slipped into comfortable, hot pink felt slippers with the same pale pink flower trim. They were designed as right and left foot styles. $150.00

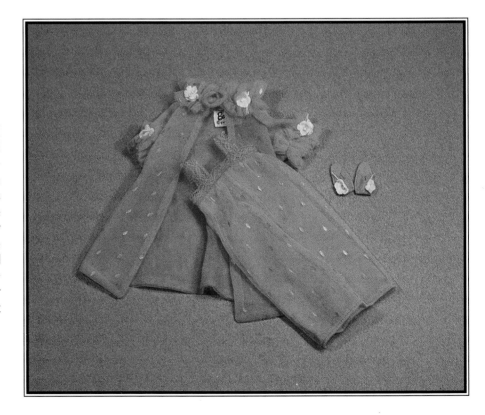

Fancy Dancy (1968 – 1969)
#1858

Barbie doll could rival any neon sign in her mod chartreuse and fuchsia jacket dress! The dress had a gathered chartreuse mini skirt at the dropped waist. The fuchsia bodice was sleeveless and featured lace trim down the front. Her chartreuse long-sleeved jacket had fuchsia piping and lace trim around the neck and down the front. The sleeves were also lace trimmed. And, the most interesting feature of the ensemble was a pair of sheer stockings with fuchsia flocked flowers and green leaves sprinkled on them! Hot pink bow shoes completed the look. $200.00

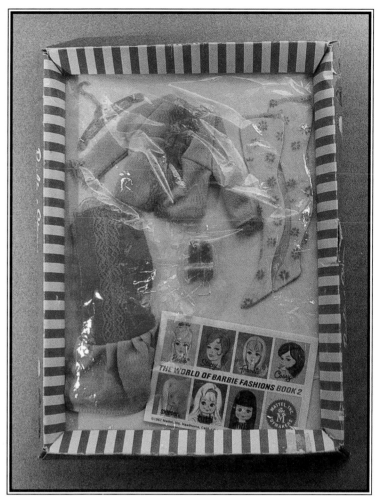

Tunic 'n Tights (1968 – 1969)
#1859

One of my personal favorites! Hot, hot pink and bright yellow striped tights and long sleeved turtleneck were the foundation of this mod outfit. Topping these pieces were textured yellow shiny vinyl shorts and a scoop neck tunic with patch pockets. These pieces were stitched in hot pink. Yellow go-go boots completed the look that could be worn in different combinations. $250.00

Smasheroo (1968 – 1969)
#1860

Barbie doll's complete winter ensemble featured a shirtdress in a red/purple/yellow/black vertical striped cotton. The dress had long sleeves, collar, and golden bead button trim at the placket and on the cuffs. A golden chain belt accented the hip line. A yellow plush cape lined with the dress fabric and plush hat plus yellow patterned hose and tall red boots completed the warm outfit Barbie doll wore to her substitute teaching assignment. $275.00

Prototypes

Shown are some variations from the norm that were products of this time period. According to designers at Mattel, a prototype is not a real prototype if it is made up in mismatched fabrics that are not true representations of what the garment is intended to look like. So, whether a fashion is a prototype or just a means to an end, both are interesting to the collector! The following 10 fashions range in value from $25.00 to $300.00.

Green top, blue belt and bubble print skirt and hat with tag.

Black polka dot dress with wide ruffle on bottom. Strapless evening gown, gold bodice, blue skirt with sheer overskirt.

Hot pink double breasted coat dress, white collar and cuffs. Strapless sundress blue bodice and tights, blue and white checked skirt and shoulder bag.

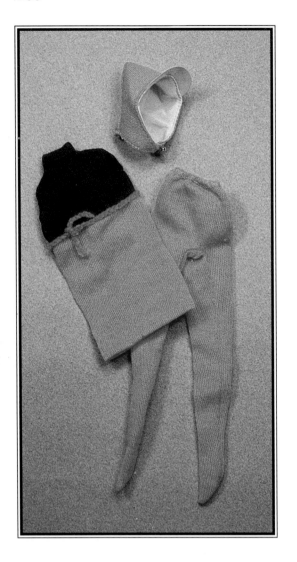

This photo features three outfits. From left to right: pink shawl and blue top and green skirt with overlay and stripes; gold dress with red leaves; gown with white long skirt and yellow top.

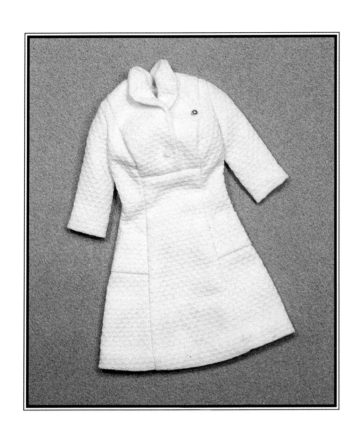

Barbie Doll Gift Sets

The Barbie doll (and friends) gift sets and exclusive outfit from 1968 were all department store exclusives for either Sears or J. C. Penney.

Sears
Travel In Style Set (1968)
#1544

This handsome gift set featured beautiful cover art of Barbie doll in motion. The doll included in the set was the standard #1190 Barbie doll in pink two-piece swimsuit with matching hair ribbon. The Sears exclusive outfit featured a royal and green floral print swing coat with green vinyl trim. This topped a royal sleeveless shell and floral mini with green vinyl waistband. Accessories were royal hose and bow shoes and a green/blue/white labeled travel hat box molded in green plastic completed the set. $1,500.00

Sears Exclusive
New Talking Barbie Doll
Dinner Dazzle Set (1968)
#1551

This gift set featured the talking Barbie doll with her exclusive Sears ensemble. This outfit utilized a beautiful pink changeable lamé for the two-piece suit. Genuine fur trimmed the neckline and a pink silk blouse with ruffled placket and pink and "diamond" shank buttons were elegant. Pink closed toe shoes and hose completed the set. $1,500.00

Sears Exclusive
Glimmer Glamour
Exclusive Outfit (1968)
#1547

This absolutely gorgeous ensemble seems elusive—probably due in part to the delicate fabrics that do not wear well. The dress was lined in blue silk and the sheer organdy overskirt and overblouse featured golden glitter dots. This organdy is extremely fragile! Golden braid accented the bottom of the bodice and a wide goldtone belt nipped in the waist. The coat was a trapeze style with a tie at the neck and ¾ sleeves. The fabric was a golden lamé knit lined in sheer yellow nylon. Golden color hose (exclusive to this set) and clear open toe shoes with golden glitter completed one of my favorite outfits. $2,000.00

Sears Exclusive
Stripes Are Happenin'
Stacey Doll Gift Set (1968)
#1545

A Twist 'n Turn Stacey doll had a wonderful mod casual outfit in bright striped knit. The mini skirt with vinyl waistband was topped by a vinyl and fabric jacket and knit top. Striped socks and hot pink go-go boots completed the set. $1,500.00

J. C. Penney Exclusive
Silver 'n Satin Set (1968)
#921-1552

This beautiful gift set featured a talking Barbie doll with her exclusive J. C. Penney outfit. The ensemble featured a mini dress with silver sleeveless top and silver and pink zig zag design lamé skirt and pink satin waistband. A pink satin coat with nylon lining and wide metallic silvertone belt at the empire waist completed the look. Accessories were a pink lacy half slip with bow accent, pink hose, silver purse, and closed toe shoes. $1,500.00

World of Barbie Doll Fashion Paks

This year there were four new fashion paks, variations of the Flats 'n Heels pak, and Fancy Trimmins' from 1967 was repeated with the name of Change-Abouts.

Flats 'n Heels (1968)

This pak contained 13 pairs of shoes for Barbie doll and her friends. These were: orange, turquoise, red, hot pink, bone, and black closed toe pumps; royal bow shoes; pink flats; cork with goldtone wedgies; and open toe pumps in white, green, turquoise, and hot pink. $75.00

Extra Casuals (1968)

This set had great summery accessories including a yellow linen hat with brim; yellow, and hot pink closed toe shoes; a pink vinyl tote with big daisy accent; pink rectangular drop earrings; and two bracelets. $75.00

Add-Ons (1968)

Fashion essentials: green and white double strand necklace; pink and red intertwined dangle earrings; wide solid pink and solid red bracelets (like Floating Gardens # 1696); golden drop triangle earrings (like Casey doll's); black plastic granny glasses; a pink vinyl shoulder bag; and pink plastic make-up kit featuring an eyelash brush, eye pencil and hand mirror! $75.00

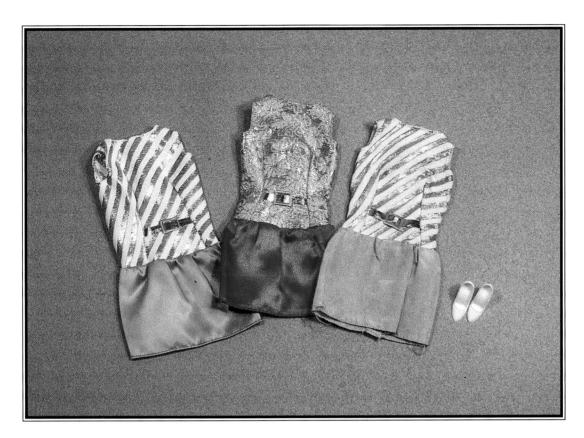

Dressed-Up! (1968)

Evening elegance in a brocade top and satin or silk skirt with golden accent belt with buckle in front of the dress. This pak came in various fabrics (as did many others). Closed toe pumps completed the look. $75.00

Pedal Pushers (1968)

Great for those casual summer days around the house! Blue chambray pedal pushers and a sleeveless blouse with yellow stitching and flats. $75.00

Francie and Casey Dolls
Fashion Pak Assortment

Three new paks were added this year and one was altered, Footnotes. The paks Hair Dos and For Francie Dressmakers were repeated.

Footnotes (1968)

The set contained white and orange pumps with cutouts; turquoise, royal, red, and pink pumps; blue buckle flats; green go-go boots; and clear with red accent boots. $75.00

Cool-It! (1968)

A cute and cool summer shift was fashioned for Francie doll in bright yellow with black and white trim. The dress was cotton and the trim was the same fabric used in Check This #1291. Two black buttons held the shoulder straps. Cute cork sandals with yellow nylon ties completed the set. Note two scales in checked fabric. $50.00

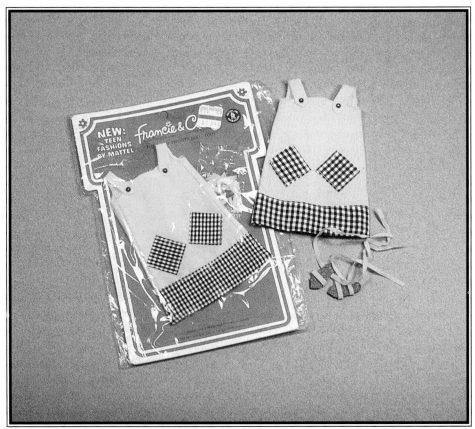

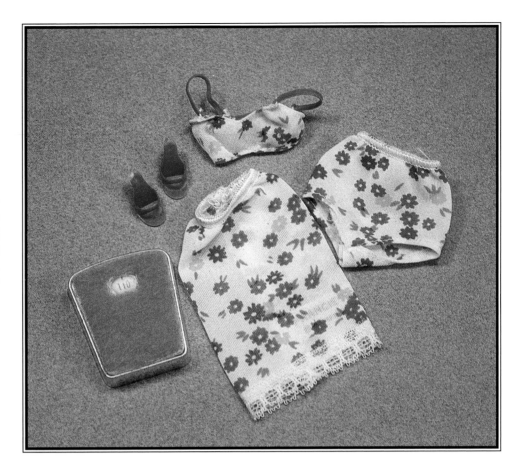

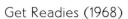

Get Readies (1968)

Francie doll chose the brightest mod lingerie in a large floral print tricot. The bra and panties were teamed with a sheath slip with lace trim. Completers were a pink fuzzy scale and shoes. $50.00

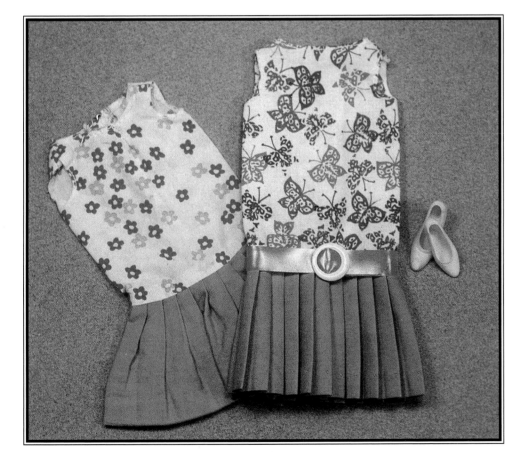

Slightly Summery (1968)

This cool sleeveless dress came in a variety of fabric combos. Shown is only a sample. The sleeveless bodice featured a dropped waist that ended at a pleated skirt. A wide vinyl belt with circular buckle and shoes completed the look. $75.00

Francie and Casey Dolls Fashion Pak Costumes

This year was exciting when it came to fashions for Francie doll! Of course her friend Casey doll and even Twiggy doll shared the fun. Twelve new outfits were added to the Ensemble Pak line, there was a new Sears exclusive, and four oufits from 1967 were repeated. These repeats were Slumber Number #1271, Hi-Teen #1272, Side-Kick! #1273, and Iced Blue #1274.

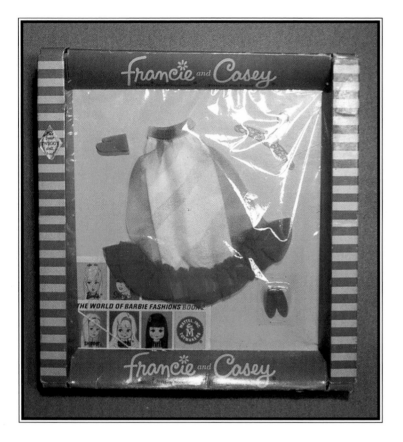

Floating In (1968 – 1969)
#1207

An airy dream of a tent dress for Francie doll. She floated into the room in the diagonally striped pastel dress with roll collar and pink ruffle at the hem. The georgette was lined with white tafetta and accessories were short, hot pink gloves and closed toe pumps. $200.00

The Silver Cage (1968 – 1969)
#1208

Francie doll was ready to disco the night away in this mod caged look! The metallic silvertone net A-line dress had silvertone braid trim at the neck and hem. It was lined with hot pink nylon. Francie doll chose hot pink/metallic silvertone stockings, hot pink bow shoes, and a metallic silvertone clutch. $250.00

Hill-riders (1968 – 1969)
#1210

Ready for the great outdoors! Francie doll looked great in a bright green, bulky knit pullover sweater with multi-color striped capris. Green go-go boots completed her look. $150.00

Mini-Chex (1968 – 1969)
#1209

A cute look in the miniest of minis! The orange and yellow checkerboard knit was outlined in white. The sleeveless dress had a wide, soft vinyl waistband with three golden bead buttons on the side. Orange and yellow striped knit knee socks, orange bow shoes, and a shiny vinyl shoulder bag completed the ensemble. $200.00

Tenterrific (1968 – 1969)
#1211

A great outfit for a beautiful day in town—shopping, of course! The predominantly chartreuse impressionistic floral dress featured lots of tiny pleats meeting the high yoke. A matching pleated scarf featured chartreuse grosgrain ribbon ties. Chartreuse patterned cotton pantyhose and bow shoes plus a white textured vinyl tote with ribbon handles and pink floral detail completed Francie doll's ensemble. $250.00

Night Blooms (1968 – 1969)
#1212

Bold but delicate! Giant wild flowers in blue and pink blossomed on the pink tricot gown with empire waist and white lace trim. The sheer tricot robe was hot pink with white lace trim at the neck, sleeves, and belted waist. A wide ruffle accented the hem. Cute, hot pink felt scuffs featured white lace and felt straps. $200.00

Pazam! (1968 – 1969)
#1213

How could any outfit better describe the mid-sixties? Geometrics! Brillant colors! See-through clothing! Pink hair! The culotte mini dress featured big yellow and hot pink dots on a chartreuse background. Francie doll's clear vinyl coat featured matching designs of clear circles within color squares. Chartreuse braid accented the neckline, long sleeves, and hem. A chartreuse two-piece swimsuit in soft vinyl, a hot pink braid hairpiece with brass barrette and chartreuse grosgrain ribbon, and green closed toe pumps with cut-outs completed the set. $300.00

Culotte-Wot? (1968 – 1969)
#1214

This cerise taffeta mini culotte set featured a white satin collar, neck tie, and faux pockets. A floppy white satin hat, white fishnet hose, tallest cerise vinyl boots, and green sunglasses with polka dot trim completed the way-out look! $300.00

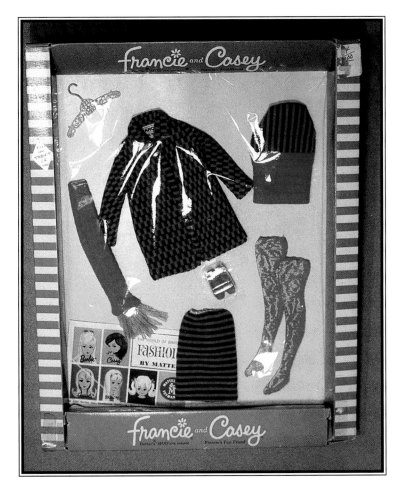

The Combo (1968)
#1215

The same knit fabric combination used in Twiggy doll's Twigster #1727 was seen in hot pink and dark blue in the combo. Francie doll's top featured a vertically striped bodice, wide, solid pink ribbed waistband, and a horizontally striped skirt. The ¾ coat with collar was fashioned from coordinating block design fabric with striped piping down the front and was lined in pink tafetta. A hot pink scarf with fringed ends, hot pink cotton lacy hose, and bow shoes completed the set. $300.00

The Lace-Pace (1968)
#1216

The perfect ensemble for the perfect party! Francie doll chose a white lace ensemble lined in gold lamé. The mini dress had an empire waistline and ruffled hem. Both were accented with hottest pink satin. The lace/lamé coat was lined with hot pink and featured a big, hot pink satin accent bow on the ruffled skirt. White fishnet hose and hot pink bow shoes completed the party set. $350.00

Dreamy Wedding (1968)
#1217

Francie doll's first wedding dress—which she only modelled, of course! The modern style featured slim A-line styling from the high yoke. The sheer sleeves echoed the slightly flared design. The gown was fashioned of a modern, daisy-embroidered organza over a satin lining with sheer organza sleeves. The tulle veil was caught with a simple satin bow. Accessories were white closed toe shoes, and a bouquet of white lace with green edging bloomed with white velvet flowers and green leaves. $375.00

Wild 'n Wooly (1968)
#1218

Truly a wild outfit! Orange satin rompers featured hot pink lace trim. The fabric for the skirt and coat was a clear vinyl base with a heavily woven multicolor surface. Orange vinyl piped the skirt's hem and waist and also trimmed the coat's neckline, sleeves, and hem. A shiny orange shoulder bag and closed toe pumps with cut-outs completed the look. $300.00

Sears Exclusive
Orange Zip (1968)

Francie doll had a single Sears exclusive outfit this year. It featured bright orange vinyl in a mini coat and dress with multicolor horizontal striped sleeveless bodice. The coat featured brass tab closures. Orange go-go boots completed the mod look. $350.00

Twiggy Doll Ensemble Paks

Francie and Casey dolls could also wear all costumes made for Twiggy doll.

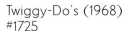

Twiggy-Do's (1968)
#1725

The top teen model stepped out in a vertical ribbed knit sleeveless dress in yellow. Horizontal green and white bands accented the hip line (and still could not make the pencil thin model look broad!!) Yellow knit knee socks, yellow bow shoes, green and white beads, and a yellow shiny vinyl shoulder bag with golden chain strap completed her ensemble. $250.00

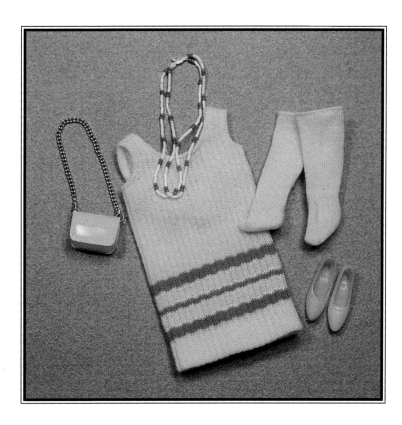

Twiggy Turnouts (1968)
#1726

A mad, mod sleeveless mini dress for evening featured a metallic fabric with a multicolor striped bodice and silvertone skirt. A wide silvertone perforated belt accented the hip line. Boots molded in gray vinyl and painted metallic silver, and a nylon bra and panty set in the same stripe design as the dress bodice completed the set. (In the 1968 Mattel catalog, the bra and panties are called a swimsuit, but don't they look like underwear?) $250.00

Twigster (1968)
#1727

Ready to go on a modelling assignment anywhere in the world—Twiggy doll's outfit featured a complete make-up kit in a cute orange plastic case that really opened. The contents were a hot pink comb, brush, and mirror set; a hot pink and white puff with ribbon handle; a black plastic eyelash brush; and a brown eye pencil. Twiggy doll's outfit featured yellow and orange print fabric fashioned into a sheath dress. The sleeveless bodice featured a block print and the skirt rose to an empire waist and had horizontal stripes. A matching block print scarf with yellow fringed ends and orange heels with cut-outs completed the model's look. $250.00

Twiggy Gear (1968)
#1728

For sightseeing on those modelling assignments, Twiggy doll wore a mod jumpsuit featuring a pink/red/white/royal horizontal striped knit sleeveless bodice with dropped waist and white vinyl slacks. A royal belt with goldtone rectangular buckle accented the suit. A pink hat with royal trim and ties with a pink plastic slide holder, royal buckle flats, and black plastic camera with gray painted trim completed the look. (The bodice fabric was the same fabric used in Barbie doll's Fashion Shiner #1691 dress.) $250.00

Skipper Doll's Ensemble Pak Costumes

Skipper doll had eight new outfits to share with Scooter doll this year. The styles were super mod with the same high quality fabrics and designs seen in the other dolls' wardrobes.

**Twist 'n Turn Skipper Doll
Original Outfit (1968)
#1105**

Her cute cotton swimsuit featured either woven or printed stripes with a pleated skirt and golden bead button trim. $45.00

**Posie Party (1968)
#1955**

Skipper doll prettied herself for Scooter doll's birthday party! She chose a predominantly blue, watercolor print dress with long sleeves and empire waist. The skirt featured a center pleat. Cuffs were lace trimmed and the waist had a hot pink nylon ribbed belt and bow. Lace trimmed hot pink taffeta petti-pants, white cotton lace pantyhose, soft hot pink flats, a chocolate sundae, and a silver metal spoon completed the party set. $200.00

Baby Dolls (1968)
#1957

Skimmy Stripes (1968)
#1956

This Skipper doll outfit would brighten any school day to the max! The brightest orange was horizontally striped with green, yellow, and hot pink. The bodice and long sleeves were orange and the neck was banded in hot pink. The accessories were the wildest! Striped knit knee socks, an orange felt hat with bill and attached chartreuse vinyl granny glasses, and orange go-go boots completed her look. For the school day, Skipper doll had a black, shiny book strap holding two books, yellow-English and green-Arithmetic and two pencils. $200.00

Skipper doll looked adorable in her pink baby doll p.j.s. The sheer pink was lined and featured a yoke above the gathered bottom. Her bloomers featured white lace trim on the legs. Lace trimmed the neckline, front, and bottom of her top. Blue braid and a hot pink bow also accented the front. Hot pink felt slippers with braid trim completed the outfit. A fuzzy scale and a comb and brush completed the set. $150.00

Patent 'n Pants (1968)
#1958

Red, white, and blue go mod in vinyl and dots! The cute jumpsuit featured blue slacks with a sleeveless, giant polka dot top in red, white, and blue. A red shiny vinyl belt with rectangular brass buckle completed the pantsuit. Skipper doll's shiny red vinyl jacket featured six goldtone bead buttons in a double breasted style. White braid accented the sleeves and the dotted fabric was used for the jacket lining. Red flats completed the look. $175.00

Warm 'n Wonderful (1968)
#1959

This great school outfit was perfect for those chilly fall days. Skipper doll's green and blue striped knit dress had a roll collar and dropped waist. A wonderful color-blocked green and blue plush coat featured green vinyl piping. Green fishnet nylon pantyhose, a blue molded vinyl cap, and blue boots completed the look. $200.00

Trim Twosome (1968)
#1960

Skipper doll's perfect-for-Easter ensemble featured a brightly striped dress in pink, orange, peach, and white. The sleeveless yoke featured three golden bead buttons. The skirt featured mini pleats. The light spring coat was white textured polyester and was fully lined in white nylon. Four golden bead buttons and a white with orange striped belt with rectangular brass buckle accented the coat. An orange vinyl bag with golden bead button and white flats completed the set. $200.00

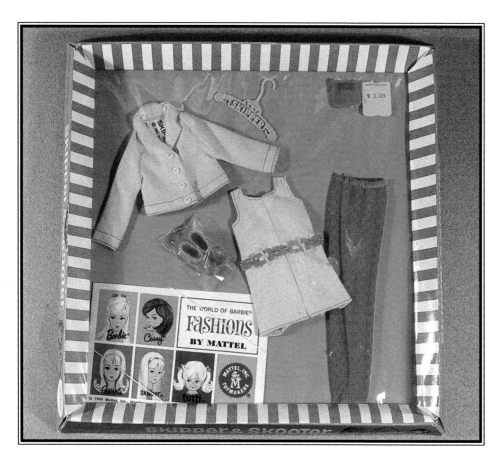

Real Sporty (1968)
#1961

As bright as a sunny day way out West! Skipper doll's bright yellow romper had a pink, plastic decorative "chain" belt and was accented with hot pink stitching as was the matching jacket. The jacket had four buttons at the closure. Hot pink cotton lace pantyhose and hot pink go-go boots completed the bright look. $200.00

Quick Change (1968)
#1962

Great mix and match pieces for wardrobe versatility! A blue sheath featured an oversize contrasting red-orange zipper. Also included was a pleated skirt in red-orange and blue. A hot pink, red, and blue color-blocked cardigan sweater featured a high collar and four golden bead buttons. Hot pink knee socks with orange tassles and hot pink go-go boots completed the set. $200.00

Two Sears Exclusives For Skipper Doll In 1968

Living Skipper Doll
Perfectly Pretty Set (1968)
#1546

A lovely Twist 'n Turn Skipper doll was featured with a coat and dress set in blue velvet. The bodice of the dress was white and was trimmed in lace and ribbon and had a pink ribbon waistband. Accessories were matching shoes and a velvet bonnet.
$1,500.00

Sears Exclusive Outfit
Confetti Cutie (1968)

Skipper doll's outfit featured a turquoise
and yellow block print knit shirt and
knee socks and a yellow jumper with
golden chain belt. A turquoise, molded
cap and yellow go-go boots completed
the ensemble. $350.00

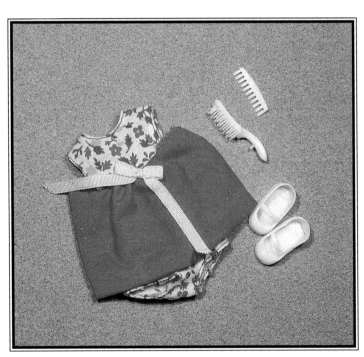

Tutti Doll
Original Outfit (1968 – 1971)
#3580

Most of the dolls wore the same dress as 1967 (rose
bodice and floral skirt) but the revised version was
switched and the latter continued as the version seen
through 1971. $25.00

Buffy And Mrs. Beasley Dolls
(1968 – 1970)
#3577

The cute T.V. star was a great companion for Tutti doll. She wore a red dotted
dress with red skirt with rickrack trim.
She had dotted panties, white tricot
socks, shoes, and carried her own Mrs.
Beasley doll with black granny glasses.
$35.00

Tutti and Chris Doll Share Four New Ensemble Paks in 1968

Sea-Shore Shorties (1968 – 1969)
#3614

The cutest little girl at the beach wore a chartreuse with blue floral print bikini. Eyelet lace trimmed both the bikini and the matching sundress. Tutti doll's adorable accessories were a beach ball, plastic sailboat, and white shoes. $125.00

Flower Girl (1968 – 1969)
#3615

Tutti doll made an adorable flower girl in her full-length blue and white gown! The bodice was sleeveless blue satin with white edging. The white taffeta skirt had an embroidered organza overskirt and turquoise ribbon trim. A blue ribbon headband hat had yellow net and floral trim. Tutti doll carried a yellow, ribbon-trimmed lace basket of yellow and blue flowers and she wore white bow shoes. $150.00

Pink P.J.'s (1968 – 1969)
#3616

Off to bed it was for tiny Tutti doll in her dreamy pink p.j.'s. The sheer pink set was lined and had a double row of white lace on the yoke, a row at the hem of the top and the pants legs. A blue rosette accented the hem of the top and tiny, pink felt slippers completed the outfit. But, how could Tutti doll fall asleep without her tiny molded plastic "frozen" baby doll in pink fleece bunting with lacy edging!? A blue comb and brush set was also included. $125.00

Birthday Beauties (1968 – 1969)
#3617

Tutti doll stole the limelight at the birthday party! She was adorable in a pink party dress splashed with pretty flowers. The long sleeved dress featured a full skirt and white fishnet tights and white shoes with straps completed her festive look. Her party accessories were a pink plate with foam cake slice with two pink painted stripes, a package wrapped in golden foil with white ribbon and a flat pink flower, a glittered pink crepe paper party favor, and a party invitation. $125.00

Chapter II – 1969

World of Barbie Doll Fashion Scene

The styles were still wonderfully mod with minis, midis and maxis abounding! Bright colors and daring prints in interesting fabrics characterized Barbie doll's wardrobe that also fit Stacey, Christie and Julia dolls. Barbie doll had 36 new outfits this year plus paks, Sears and J. C. Penney sets. Sixteen were repeated from 1968. The repeats were Knit Hit #1804, Zokko! #1820, Underliners #1821, Swirly-Cue #1822, Snug Fuzz #1813, Sparkle Squares #1814, All That Jazz #1848, Wedding Wonder #1849, Now Wow! #1853, Twinkle Togs #1854, Team Ups #1855, Wild 'n Wonderful #1856, Dreamy Pink #1857, Fancy Dancy #1858, Tunic 'n Tights #1859, and Smasheroo #1860.

Original Outfits for Barbie Dolls and Friends from 1969

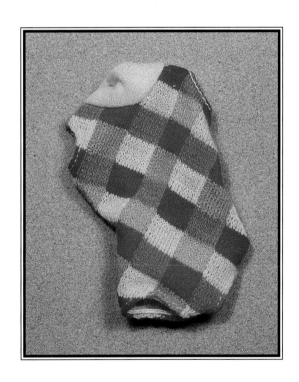

Twist 'n Turn Barbie Doll
Original Outfit (1969)
#1160

Barbie doll's new one-piece knit suit was fashioned from colorful checked cloth with a yellow neck band. $35.00

Talking Barbie Doll
Original Outfit (1969)
#1115

Late in the year, the doll wore a two-piece red-orange vinyl swimsuit and lacy cover-up with vinyl trim. There was a floral lace version of the suit featuring a melon vinyl suit and trim. $35.00

Talking P. J. Doll
Original Outfit (1969)
#1113

Truly mod! P.J.'s groovy print tricot mini dress had bell sleeves, matching lace trimmed pink panties, and chunky shoes. $35.00

Twist 'n Turn Stacey Doll
Original Outfit (1969)
#1165

Stacey doll's one-piece jersey multicolor suit featured a wide white neck band. $35.00

Talking Truly Scrumptious Doll
Original Outfit (1969)
#1107

The talking doll wore a bright pink satin, pale pink satin and black net with flocked dots dress with matching hat with marabou trim. Palest pink chunky shoes completed her ensemble. $150.00

Standard Truly Scrumptious Doll
Original Outfit (1969)
#1108

A truly lovely doll and ensemble! The long, palest pink dress featured a lace overdress, puffed sleeves, and ruffled hem with a satin ribbon at the waist. Her big picture hat had floral trim and spring green tulle that accented the hat and tied under her chin. Palest pink chunky shoes completed the look. $150.00

Make Mine Midi (1969)
#1861

Not shown in any booklet or dealer catalog, this outfit is easy to miss but is a nice addition to the mod midi skirt era. A white, lace-trimmed blouse with two goldtone bead buttons tucked into the pink skirt that was sprinkled with 3D nylon flowers and had a yellow velvet waistband. Pink hose, chunky shoes, and a half slip completed the set. $250.00

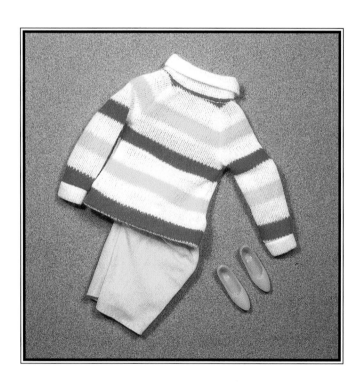

Country Capers (1969)
#1862

The brightly colored sweater featured yellow, orange, and white stripes with white roll collar and cuffs. Yellow Bermuda shorts and flat shoes completed the set Barbie doll loved for those early spring days in the country! $150.00

Pretty Power (1969)
#1863

Barbie and Stacey dolls looked equally lovely in this prim and proper top with attached mod mini skirt! The long sleeved white top had sheer ruffle trim at the neck, down the front and on the cuffs. The front was accented by two pink shank buttons with a "diamond" set. Black elastic formed the waistband above the floral swirls on the pink, whipped cream skirt. Black bow shoes completed the look. $150.00

Close-Ups (1969)
#1864

Bright underthings were the perfect foundation for Barbie doll's mod wardrobe. Her hot pink cotton lace bra had a yellow flower accent. The pantyhose had a cotton lace panty also with floral trim with hot pink hose. Her two-tiered mini petticoat was sheer yellow nylon with hot pink tulle trim. Truly electric! $150.00

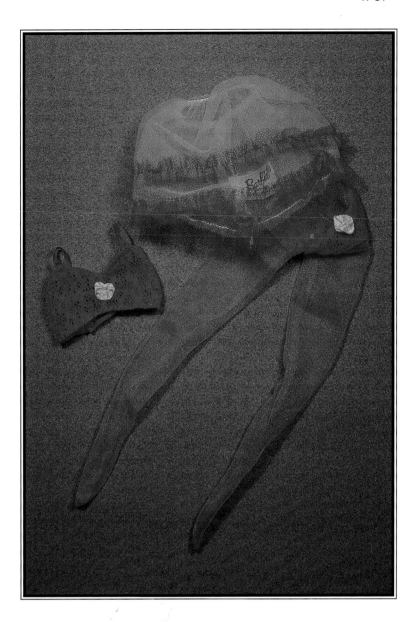

Glo-Go (1969)
#1865

Ready for the dance floor, Barbie doll twirled in swirls of chiffon and metallic knit. The halter top featured a high collar and matching belt at the empire waist. The fabric was a raspberry metallic knit. The white chiffon skirt was swirled with raspberry and sprinkled with dots. The skirt was lined with white satin. Raspberry chunky shoes completed the stunning set. $200.00

Movie Groovie (1969)
#1866

Barbie doll wanted to wear something memorable to the movie premiere. She chose a hot pink and "silver" look. Her long top was a silver lamé vest look with attached sheer, hot pink long sleeves and ruffled V neck. Her A-line hot pink skirt, hose, and bow shoes completed the set. $150.00

Dream-Ins (1969)
#1867

A shorty nightie in sheer hot pink fabric lined in orange nylon with a lace bodice, ribbon straps, and back tie at the empire waist. The plush robe was in matching hot pink and had lace trim, satin ties, and seam binding. $150.00

Happy Go Pink (1969)
#1868

This pretty party dress featured a hot pink organza bodice with ¾ sleeves and roll collar. The bodice had a strapless lace-trimmed pink satin lining. The organza skirt had hot pink embroidery and was lined with white taffeta. An attached metallic silvertone belt and pink chunky shoes completed the set. $150.00

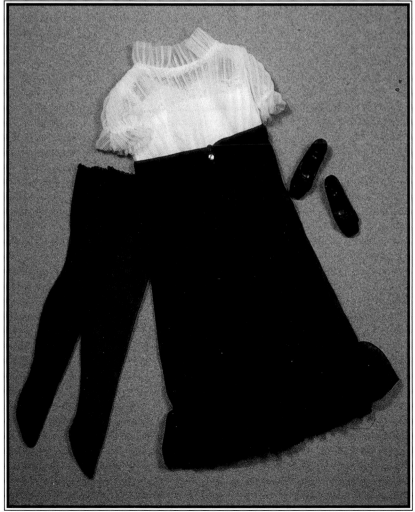

Midi-Magic (1969)
#1869

This beautiful romantic dress was a little old-fashioned and a little mod! The bodice was fashioned of a textured stripe sheer fabric and white strapless lace-trimmed taffeta lining. The dress featured a stand-up collar and short sleeves. The black organza skirt had a ruffled hem and was lined with black taffeta with lace trim on the hem. A velvet ribbon belt at the empire waist had two black shank buttons with "diamond" sets as accents. Black sheer hose and bow shoes completed the set. $250.00

Midi-Marvelous (1969)
#1870

The perfect portrait dress for an old-fashioned girl! This sweet white organdy dress featured embroidered borders on the double tiered skirt, the gathered ¾ sleeves, and at the neck. The dress featured a white satin lining. Pink ribbon formed the waistband and rosettes on the sleeves. The matching hat had the embroidered fabric for the brim and a pink ribbon hatband. White bow shoes and white stockings completed the late '60s Plantation Belle look! $250.00

Romantic Ruffles (1969)
#1871

Barbie doll looked her radiant best in this pink and silver evening dress. The silvery lamé over the pink, sleeveless bodice met a five tiered pink net skirt sparkled with silver dots. The ruffles had a sheer lining and a hot pink taffeta underskirt. A pink satin ribbon and a net and taffeta flower accented the empire waist. Mod rosette earrings of sheer pink fabric and a silvertone bead on chains hung to Barbie doll's shoulders. A clutch bag was fashioned of the silvery lamé and was lined in the pink taffeta. It closed with a silvertone bead button. Pink bow shoes completed the ensemble. $300.00

See-Worthy (1969)
#1872

The bright turquoise sailor dress featured great nautical styling. The middy blouse top featured yellow soutache braid on the collar and cuffs. The front sported yellow buttons. A yellow satin ribbon tied at the neck. The pleated skirt met the dropped waist and fell to midi length. Turquoise knit knee highs featured yellow soutache trim. Her nautical tam featured braid trim, too, and a cute yellow pom pon. Matching turquoise tennis shoes and a black plastic camera with painted gray trim completed the set. $250.00

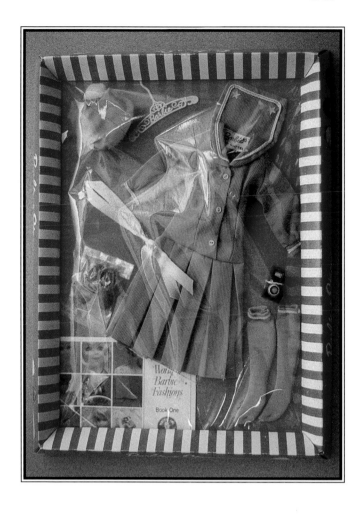

Plush Pony (1969)
#1873

Fake fur was never wilder and warmer! Barbie doll's dress featured an electric orange top with collar and black and white faux fur skirt. Orange vinyl piped the hem. A metallic goldtone attached belt accented the waist. The furry coat featured orange vinyl piping on the neckline, front and sleeves. A goldtone chain belt held the coat together. Orange mid-calf vinyl boots completed the set. $250.00

Fab City (1969)
#1874

This floral fantasy could only have been conceived in the late '60s! The rich silvertone lamé bodice featured silvertone spaghetti straps. The wild 3D flowers of sheer pink were sprinkled on the floral printed organdy skirt. Bold black rays exploded from the flowers. The underskirt was fashioned of white satin and the waist had a rose satin waistband. The matching stole was silvertone lamé with a rose satin lining. The set was completed with short, pink tricot gloves and cut-out shoes. $300.00

Let's Have A Ball (1969)
#1879

This outfit was truly set for any ball Barbie doll chose! The rich, turquoise velvet sleeveless bodice met a soft turquoise organza overskirt with a delicate floral print. The waist was accented by a golden waistband and tie with a golden floral brooch with a purplish pink stone set. The skirt was lined with white satin. For a chilly evening, Barbie doll had a matching velvet jacket with full sleeves. The jacket featured a white, genuine fur collar and was lined in white satin. Pale blue closed toe shoes completed the ensemble. $300.00

Winter Wedding
(1969 – 1970)
#1880

Beautiful, heavy brocade was fashioned into Barbie doll's winter wedding fantasy. The dress had a fitted bodice
with long sleeves. Rabbit fur trimmed the neck-
line and cuffs. The flared skirt featured two front pleats at the waist and a braid-edged scalloped hem. A train
fell from the neckline. The headpiece was fashioned from the brocade and was trimmed in fur with a tulle veil
attached. A big bouquet of green-edged lace with five pink velvet flowers and green leaves was tied with satin
ribbon. White closed toe shoes completed the set. $350.00

Made For Each Other (1969)
#1881

Barbie doll chose coordinates that matched from head to toe! A yellow knit sleeveless blouse was topped by a loosely woven mini skirt of yellow, white, and orange with orange satin ribbon waistband. The mini skirt was topped by a midi coat made of the same fabric with a big orange plush collar and a wide, shiny vinyl belt with goldtone circular buckle. Her accessories were a matching plush hat, yellow and orange double strand of plastic beads, and tall orange boots. $350.00

Silver Sparkle (1969)
#1885

This evening mini featured a ribbed silver lamé bodice with long sleeves. The dropped torso met a metallic silver knit A-line skirt. A bow adorned the waist. Clear cut-out shoes completed the ensemble. $200.00

Salute To Silver
(1969 – 1970)
(same outfit as #1885)

The same dress (with clear open toe shoes) found in Ensemble Pak #1885 was available through the introductory promo set for the new *Barbie Talk* magazine. Also included in the set was the premier issue of the magazine, and a "signed by the dolls" group illustration of the current dolls. Some sets had the misprinted picture with two signatures transposed. $200.00 set. $300.00 w/rare photo

Hooray For Leather (1969 – 1970)
#1477

This cute twosome for daytime wear featured a yellow vinyl skirt with red-orange plush border. The bright red orange top featured plush trim on the ¾ sleeves. Yellow bow shoes completed the casual outfit. $175.00

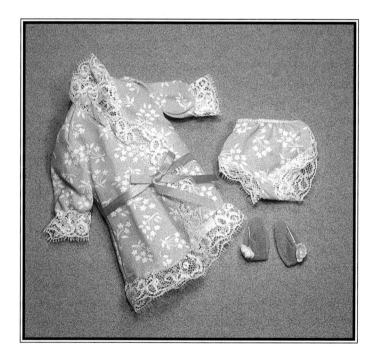

Dream Wrap (1969 – 1970)
#1476

Dreamy pink with white floral print wrapped into cute lace-trimmed shorty pajamas. A hot pink ribbon tied at the waist. Matching panties and hot pink felt slippers with floral trim completed the set. (There was a left and a right shoe!) $150.00

Shift Into Knit (1969 – 1970)
#1478

Barbie doll's knit shift featured a red bodice knit into a navy skirt. The sleeveless style was accented by a swingy, fringe-trimmed red scarf. A golden chain belt and red chunky shoes completed the set. $175.00

Leisure Leopard (1969 – 1970)
#1479

This hostess ensemble was fashioned in leopard print tricot with a yellow panel in front. Although it has the appearance of being a dress, it is really hostess pajamas. Yellow open toe pumps completed the set. $150.00

Firelights (1969 – 1970)
#1481

These evening pajamas sparkled in the firelight! The blue and silver lamé featured a paisley print. Metallic braid trimmed the wide legs and metallic silver straps accented the shoulders. Blue open toe shoes completed the ensemble. $175.00

Important In-Vestment (1969 – 1970)
#1482

A long sleeved, bright green knit mini sheath featured a golden chain belt with red flower drop. A curly faux fur vest was lined with yellow calico or solid red and fastened at the flower trim. Green chunky shoes completed the versatile look. $150.00

Little Bow Pink (1969 – 1970)
#1483

This cute little girl look featured hot pink satin in a long sleeved, empire waist style. Nylon ruffles accented the neck and sleeves. Hot pink lacy stockings and chunky shoes accessorized the dress perfectly. $150.00

Yellow Mellow (1969 – 1970)
#1484

A soft color in a soft fabric! Butter yellow velour was fashioned into a long sleeved dress. Braid trimmed the hem and formed a high collar. Sheer yellow stockings and chunky shoes completed the pretty ensemble. $150.00

Winter Wow (1969 – 1970)
#1486

The day couldn't be bleak when Barbie doll wore this good-looking suit. The bittersweet pleated mini skirt was topped by a fitted jacket. Brown fake fur trimmed the jacket neckline, placket, hem, and sleeves. There were three golden bead buttons and a metallic gold plastic belt. Accessories were a faux fur bonnet with golden braid ties, faux fur muff and gold knit fabric hip boots. $250.00

Shirtdressy (1969 – 1970)
#1487

This feminine and dressy shirt-waist was fashioned of yellow organza and had a separate matching satin slip. Five "pearls" accented the front and the full skirt was covered with lace (two skirt variations shown). Yellow chunky shoes completed the look. $150.00

Velvet Venture (1969 – 1970)
#1488

A pretty color combo in a textured blend of fabrics. The sleeveless sheath dress was fashioned of a gold and hot pink lamé. The neckline was trimmed with golden braid. The contrasting floral textured velvet coat featured silk lapels with golden braid edging and a double golden bead and chain at the closure. The sleeves also featured golden braid trim. Chartreuse chunky shoes and stockings completed the ensemble. $250.00

Cloud 9 (1969 – 1970)
#1489

Maxi and mini lengths for Barbie doll were designed into this dream time fashion. The shorty gown featured a hot pink satin yoke and a blue tricot scalloped skirt with matching panties. The peignoir had a satin stand-up yoke. The sheer blue nylon was lined in satin and the sheer sleeves were puffed. A pretty blue satin bow accented the bodice closure. Hot pink satin booties were detailed with sheer blue ruffles around the tops. $200.00

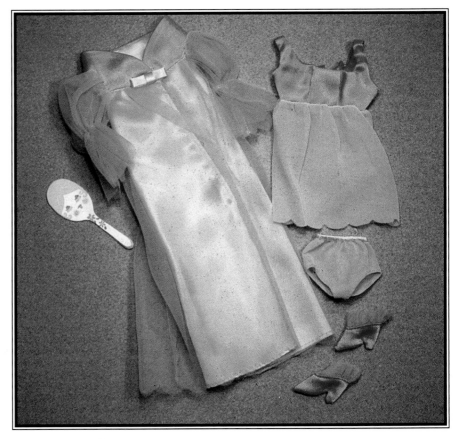

Red, White 'n Warm (1969 – 1970)
#1491

Ready to meet the winter weather with style, Barbie doll chose a cute, sleeveless color-block dress in orange and hot pink fleece. The waist was nipped with elastic. The white textured vinyl coat had a big fake fur collar and cuffs. A tab fastened at the neck with golden bead buttons. A self belt with oval buckle, matching knee-high boots with fake fur trim, and ankle chains completed the fashionable ensemble. $250.00

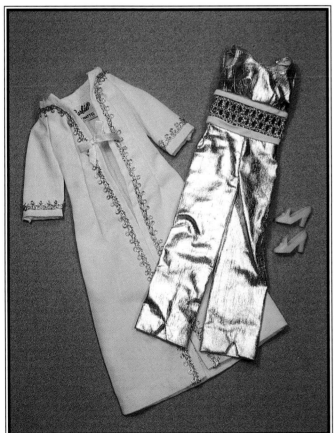

Silver Polish (1969 – 1970)
#1492

A new twist for the evening scene! Barbie doll looked smashing in a silver tricot jumpsuit with sleeveless bodice, filigree waistband, and notched pants legs. An elegant long evening coat of yellow faille was generously trimmed with metallic silver braid. Chunky yellow shoes completed the set. $250.00

Fab Fur (1969 – 1970)
#1493

This gorgeous fake fur suit featured a mini skirt topped by a hot pink satin lined jacket held at the waist with a golden chain and bead buttons. A sleeveless hot pink blouse featured golden trim which matched the "boots" which were really golden knit footed pants! $250.00

Goldswinger (1969 – 1970)
#1494

Red-orange electric bolts flashed across a golden lamé fabric. The midi length coat was belted with a wide golden plastic belt held with two golden bead buttons and was lined in orange organdy. The dress featured a sleeveless golden knit bodice with empire waist. The ruffled red-orange organza skirt was lined with matching satin. Orange chunky shoes completed the swinging look Barbie doll loved. $250.00

Barbie Doll's Six New Paks for 1969

Flats 'n Heels (1969)

The pak included red-orange, royal, hot pink, and pale blue bow shoes; white, hot pink, and turquoise chunky shoes; red-orange and yellow go-go boots; and blue tennis shoes. $75.00

Tour-Ins (1969)

Great travel accessories included a green plastic hatbox with a green, navy, and white label; red closed umbrella with white handle; red purse with golden bead button at the closure; black camera with gray painted trim; pink sunglasses; green and white beads; and chartreuse bow shoes. $75.00

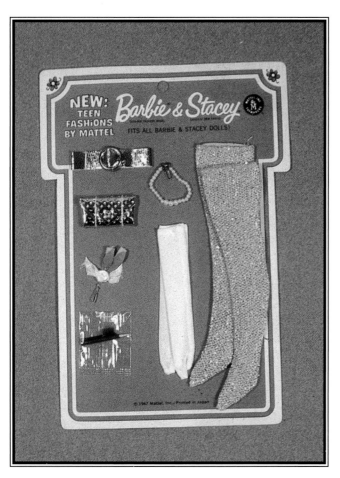

Finishing Touches (1969)

Pretty accessories for an evening out included silvery stockings, long, white tricot gloves; graduated "pearl" necklace; silvery clutch; white corsage with satin ribbon; silvery belt; black eyelash brush and eye pencil. $75.00

Petti-Pinks (1969)

The pretty pink slip had a wide, hot pink lace ruffle and silvery bow accent. Also included were felt slippers with sheer nylon bows on top; paper face mirror; pink fuzzy topped scale; golden (paper) talc box; pink and white puff; and pink comb and brush. $75.00

Terrific Twosome (1969)

The neat, sleeveless blouse in this set was paired with a gathered skirt with black velvet waistband. Closed toe pumps and a necklace were also included. Shown are variations. $75.00

Sun-Shiner (1969)

The sleeveless, A-line dress featured a cute knee-tickling ruffle at the hemline. Contrasting closed toe pumps were included. Color variations are shown. $75.00

Department Store Exclusives for 1969

There were two Sears gift sets for Barbie doll in 1969. One was an exclusive for Barbie doll alone and the other featured both Barbie and Ken dolls in a fabulous set. There was also one gift set for Barbie doll from J. C. Penney. And, Stacey doll had a glamorous gift set of her very own.

J. C. Penney Exclusive
Pink Premiere Set (1969 – 1970)
#1596

A lovely Talking Barbie doll was included with a golden lamé trimmed pink satin coat with a pretty pink, gold, and white party dress. The top of the dress was pink satin and had a multi-tiered pleated nylon skirt with pink edging over a satin overskirt. Golden braid accented the empire waist. Pink pantyhose, golden nylon gloves, golden-trimmed satin purse, and chunky shoes completed the set. $1,500.00

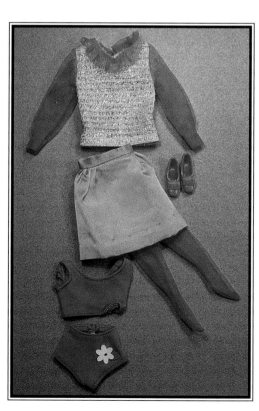

Sears Exclusive
Twinkle Town Gift Set (1969)
#1592

The #1190 Barbie doll was dressed in a blue version of her original two-piece swimsuit. The extra outfit included here was Movie Groovie #1866, so the only exclusive component of this set was the swimsuit. $1,500.00

Sears Exclusive
Stacey Doll
Nite Lightning Gift Set (1969)
#1591

The beautiful Twist 'n Turn doll had a spectacular evening ensemble featuring an evening dress with pink satin bodice and multicolor striped eyelash fabric skirt. A blue satin waistband had a nylon flower accent with "diamond". The beautiful satin evening coat had a goldtone flower brooch with a "diamond". Blue hose and bow shoes completed the gift set. $1,500.00

Sears Exclusive
Golden Groove Set (1969)
#1593

Talking Barbie doll looked elegant in her gold and pink lamé dinner suit with genuine fur trim on the sleeves. The front featured chain and golden bead buttons in a double-breasted arrangement. Golden nylon boots completed the set. $1,500.00

Sears Exclusive
Talking Barbie And Ken
Fabulous Formal Gift Set (1969)
#1595

Talking Barbie and Ken dolls wore their swimsuits and had beautiful evening ensembles that were yellow versions of Romantic Ruffles #1871 and Guruvy Formal #1431. Barbie doll's gown featured yellow in place of the pink ruffles and the accent belt was red-orange. Her drop earrings, bag, and chunky shoes were yellow. Ken doll's tuxedo jacket was yellow faille rather than red. The vest, shirt, slacks, shoes, and socks were the same as Guruvy Formal. $3,000.00

Ken Doll Was Back with A Wardrobe of Four Outfits!

More handsome than ever (and a lot more talkative!), Ken doll reappeared after his hiatus since 1967. He came in a swimsuit and shirt and had an updated wardrobe of four regular line outfits and a variation of Guruvy Formal appeared in the Fabulous Formal Gift Set #1595.

It is important to note that the shirts and jackets feature openings in the back of the neck to accommodate the talking ring and pull string! The clothing still had nice detailing such as working zippers. Since the newly styled Ken doll was larger than the original Ken doll, the clothing was sized up and larger shoe molds were used.

Talking Ken Doll
Original Outfit (1969)
#1111

Red lightweight twill formed Ken doll's swim trunks and his raglan sleeved, Nehru collar shirt. Three buttons accented the front closure. $35.00

Breakfast At 7 (1969 – 1970)
#1428

Ken doll slept well in a pair of handsome yellow pajamas with a narrow, two-tone orange check. The p.j.s were convertible to a shorter length with the solid orange trunks also included. Ken doll's orange fleece robe was trimmed with the checked fabric. A tie belt cinched at the waist. His "leather" scuffs were fashioned of a brown plastic and were a slip-on style with straps across the tops of the feet. A gray plastic shaver with plastic-covered wire "cord" completed the set. $200.00

Rally Gear (1969 – 1970)
#1429

The mod leather jacket look was accomplished in Ken doll's vinyl, double-breasted waist-length style. A long sleeved striped shirt and tan zippered slacks were completed with a pair of brown vinyl cowboy boots. $200.00

Town Turtle (1969 – 1970)
#1430

Ken doll looked especially handsome in his mod Edwardian style suit. A soft white, long sleeved Nehru shirt was paired with a handsome pair of blue mini checked slacks with zipper. The unlined double-breasted blue jacket featured wide lapels and pocket tabs. Blue knit socks and black shoes completed the set. $200.00

Guruvy Formal (1969)
#1431

Barbie doll's handsome and
guruvy boyfriend was a perfect
escort in this modern tuxedo. Ken
doll's long sleeved shirt featured a high
collar with a gold and white lamé striped
cravat (attached). White slacks with zipper, a handsome red brocade floral vest with solid red back, and a red
faille Nehru jacket completed the outfit. White socks and shoes accessorized the look. $250.00

Julia Doll's Exclusive Outfits from 1969

Julia, the beautiful television star portrayed by Diahann Carol on the series named "Julia", had four Ensemble Pak outfits designed just for her this year. These outfits, the dolls' original outfits, and the Sears gift set fashion featured a Julia doll garment label sewn into them.

Twist 'n Turn Julia Doll
Original Outfit (1969)
#1127

The T.V. star wore a two-piece
nurse's uniform with button trim and a nurse's pin. Her nurse's cap featured black braid trim and she wore white chunky shoes. $45.00

Talking Julia Doll
Original Outfit (1969 – 1971)
#1128

This glamorous jumpsuit featured gold and silver striped glitter knit, full legs, and high collar. A self belt with metal buckle accented the waist. Clear chunky shoes with molded-in glitter completed her original outfit. $45.00

Leather Weather (1969 – 1970)
#1751

A pink knit shell was topped by a heavily textured plaid mini skirt with red leather-look waistband. The coat was fashioned of the red leather-look vinyl and featured golden bead buttons at the double-breasted front closure. Red chunky shoes and a leather-look vinyl bag with one golden bead button completed the look. $200.00

Brr-Furr (1969 – 1970)
#1752

This beautiful jacket dress featured a silk, sleeveless tucked front bodice with a textured skirt and vinyl waistband. The matching jacket had a furry look collar and front accent. A vinyl belt attached to the front cinched the waist. Accessories were a matching furry hat and chunky shoes. Two color variations are shown with the pink being far less common. Julia doll's costumes had her own packaging as did Twiggy and Miss America dolls, but the pink variation here is in Barbie doll packaging but is labelled Brr-Furr #1752! $200.00

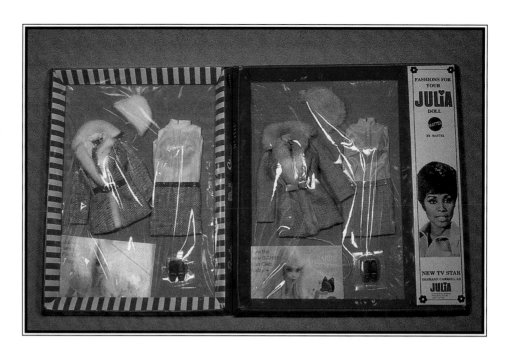

Pink Fantasy (1969 – 1970)
#1754

Julia doll looked radiant in her peignoir set. A rose tricot gown featured a lacy bodice. The sleeveless robe had an empire waist and three tiers of nylon in coordinating shades forming the skirt. A pink nylon rosette and ribbon tie accented the bodice. Golden knit booties with nylon pom pons completed the dramatic ensemble. $200.00

Candlelight Capers (1969 – 1970)
#1753

Beautiful, golden knit fabric and velvet formed the sleeveless, dropped waist sheath. Gold braid accented the waist and a velvet cape was elegantly trimmed in braid and had three golden bead buttons at the neckline and one at each tab. A feathery hat (actually velvet with a genuine fur brim) and chunky shoes completed the ensemble. $200.00

Sears Exclusive
Simply Wow Set (1969)
#1594

This wonderful set is the one and only Julia doll gift set and featured the Talking Julia doll in her original costume. The exclusive outfit was an attractive turquoise jacket dress featuring a white satin bodice and golden braid trim. Two large golden bead buttons accented the jacket closure. Matching chunky shoes completed the set. $2,000.00

Francie and Casey Dolls Ensemble Paks

Francie and Casey dolls had 16 new Ensemble Paks that they could share with Twiggy doll. Besides these new costumes, eight costumes were repeated from 1968. These were Floating In #1207, The Silver Cage #1208, Mini Chex #1209, Hill-Riders #1210, Tenterrific #1211, Night Blooms #1212, Pazam! #1213, Culotte-Wot? #1214.

Twist 'n Turn
Francie Doll (1969)
#1170

The cute doll wore a one-piece knit swimsuit with solid pink torso and striped pink and yellow bottom. $50.00

Somethin' Else (1969 – 1970)
#1219

A bright and perky yellow and hot pink floral print body blouse featured long sleeves, collar, and a single yellow button at the placket. The solid yellow cotton A-line skirt sported six hot pink buttons—three on either side of the waist. Yellow buckle flats completed Francie doll's perky set! $150.00

Land Ho! (1969 – 1970)
#1220

Nautical in a not-so-traditional way! The bright red-orange polished cotton dress was accented with turquoise. The dress had a middy blouse style collar trimmed in turquoise braid, double breasted front with six turquoise shank buttons and dropped waist. The mini A-line skirt had a pleat at the closure. A turquoise satin ribbon tie at the neck, a cute matching cap with turquoise braid and single button accent, and aqua buckle flats completed the seaworthy set. $150.00

Tennis Time (1969 – 1970)
#1221

Ready for the courts, Francie doll met her opponent in a bright white tennis dress in textured cotton. The sleeveless A-line style had matching shorts. Both pieces featured open work braid detailing. A tan tennis racquet with black handle grip and plastic strings, a white hard plastic tennis ball, and white tennis shoes completed the set. $150.00

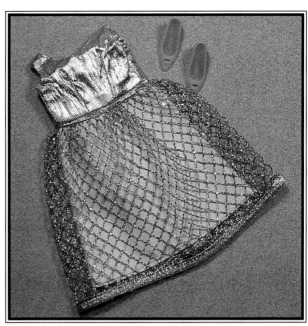

The Yellow Bit (1969)
#1223

An absolutely adorable A-line mini dress! The simple lines of the dress were accented by huge puffed sleeves. The lightweight cotton fabric was lined in cotton. The neckline was edged in turquoise braid and flower appliques danced on the airy sleeves. The underskirt was edged with the same turquoise floral braid and peeked from beneath the overskirt which was edged with the simple braid used at the neck. Pretty, light blue textured nylon hose and matching buckle flats completed the appealing ensemble. $175.00

Gold Rush (1969 – 1970)
#1222

Party pretty! Francie doll danced in this swingy mini dress! The golden metallic knit empire bodice met a bright orange satin skirt. A golden cage overskirt was trimmed with braid at the waist and the hem. Pretty orange heels with cut-outs helped Francie doll dance 'til she almost dropped! $175.00

Vested Interest (1969)
#1224

An interesting plaid in white, hot pink, pink, and yellow added interest to this conservative style. The dress featured a long sleeved top with collar that met a slim, plaid skirt. A hot pink crocheted vest or matching plaid vest featured four golden bead buttons at the closure. Heels with cut-outs completed Francie doll's ensemble. $150.00

Snazz (1969)
#1225

This snazzy mini was whipped up in pastel pink, orange, and white vertical stripes. The soft style featured ¾ puffed sleeves, a dropped waist and gathered skirt. Special interest was added to the placket with three, pink flat flower buttons with yellow bead centers and a wide pink satin ribbon sash at the dropped waist. Underneath it all, Francie doll wore a hot pink tricot bodysuit with orange lace trim and ribbon shoulder straps. Hot pink heels completed the set. $175.00

Snooze News (1969)
#1226

Francie doll's pretty soft melon sheer nightie was lined in matching tricot. The gown was accented with frilly ruffles at the bodice and a single ruffle at the hem. The bodice was accented with orange shoulder straps and a bow plus a yellow flower with orange bead center at the empire waist. The matching simple robe had a flowing collar, ruffled hem, ruffle top pocket, and ribbon tie at the neck with a single yellow flower with orange bead center. Francie doll slipped into her comfy orange felt slippers with sheer ruffles. A cardboard mirror with mod face design and metallic paper "mirror", comb and brush completed the ensemble. $150.00

Long On Looks (1969)
#1227

Fashion took a midi turn for Francie doll! Her white textured blouse featured long raglan sleeves with gathered cuffs, placket front, and collar. The ruffled tuxedo front featured green stitching and large "pearl" buttons. The pink midi skirt was fashioned from a novelty floral fabric in a combination of sheer and heavy weaves. Two skirt examples are shown here; one skirt is textured and one is not. A chartreuse satin ribbon waistband was accented with a bow in front. Accessories were a pink tricot slip with nylon cord accent bow at the ruffled hem, pink nylon fishnet stockings, and pink bow flats. $200.00

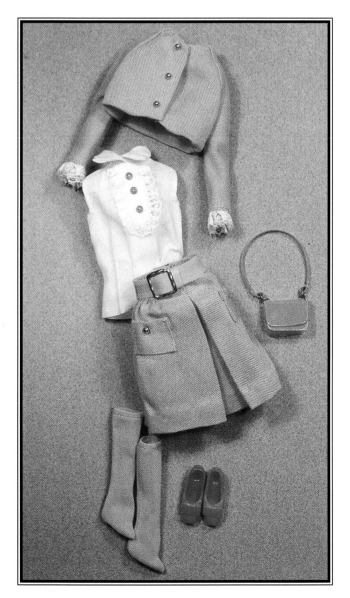

Sissy Suits (1969)
#1228

Perfect for a day of shopping with Barbie doll, Francie doll's twill suit featured a cropped box jacket with long raglan sleeves and three golden bead buttons at the front closure. White lace peeked from under the cuffs, simulating a long sleeved blouse underneath. Actually, the white blouse was sleeveless with a collar, lace trim on the front and three hot pink buttons. The modified mini skirt featured a single front pleat, two patch pockets with golden bead buttons, yellow vinyl belt with pink stripe, and a square golden buckle. Pink tricot knee socks, vinyl shoulder bag, and bow shoes completed the ensemble. $225.00

Sugar Sheers (1969)
#1229

A sheer delight for a summer day, this white lawn dress featured long white sleeves with floral fabric cuffs and a front pleat meeting the white yoke. The rows of multi-color flowers encircled the body of the dress. The sheer dress had a matching white slip with lace trim. Pink fishnet stockings, pink buckle flats, a clear plastic tote with two rows of lace, and a hot pink, blue, and white record player with Barbie label black plastic record were the accessories. $225.00

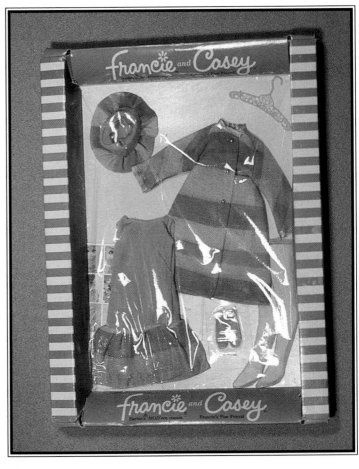

Merry-Go-Rounders (1969)
#1230

Around and around go the colorful stripes on this lightweight gauze dress and coat set. The sleeve-less dress featured a solid chartreuse bodice with dropped waist. The gathered skirt swirled ih multi-color stripes. Francie doll's matching coat featured chartreuse satin trim at the neck and cuffs. Three golden bead buttons accented the front. Her cute hat featured a solid chartreuse crown and striped brim. Chartreuse nylon stockings and bow shoes completed the set. $225.00

Pink Lightning (1969 – 1970)
#1231

Francie doll looked like she walked right off
Carnaby Street in this super mod ensemble! Her
mini jumpsuit was the hottest pink textured knit.
The sleeveless suit featured two golden chains
attached at each end to hot pink shank buttons
with "diamond" sets. Her vinyl coat coordinated
in hot pink and orange. The coat had two pocket
tabs and was lined in pink nylon. A cute matching
cap was fashioned of the pantsuit material with
orange and hot pink vinyl trim. Hot pink stockings, go-go boots, and green sunglasses with hot
pink trim completed the fantastic outfit. $250.00

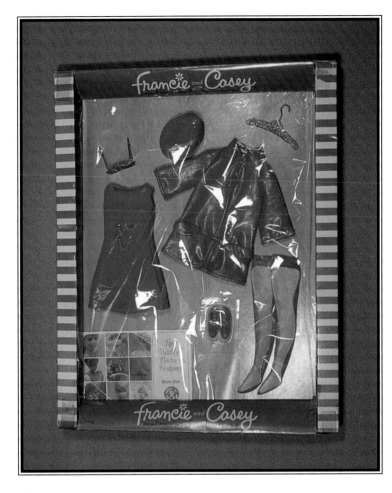

Two For The Ball (1969 – 1970)
#1232

A sophisticated color combo was fashioned into
a sweet teenage design for this Francie doll formal. Her evening gown featured a black velvet
sleeveless bodice with a pink satin underskirt and
lacy skirt. A hot pink satin waistband cinched the
waist. Her matching coat was fashioned of pink
chiffon with a lined bodice and long sleeves.
Accents were a black velvet waistband with bow.
The bow featured a single pink satin rose bud
with a green leaf. Three pink shank buttons with
"diamond" sets accented the closure, The hem
and the cuffs featured a horizontal tuck. Accessories were a black velvet covered brass headband and hot pink heels with cut-outs. $250.00

Victorian Wedding (1969 – 1970)
#1233

Francie doll made the picture perfect bride in this pure white all-over lace bridal gown. The fitted bodice featured leg-of-mutton lace sleeves. The full skirt was floor length. A white satin headpiece was held in place with a white grosgrain ribbon covered headband and had a tulle veil. The bouquet featured five velvety flowers with "pearl" centers, a froth of green tulle and white satin ribbon bow. White heels with cut-outs completed the ensemble. $300.00

The Combination (1969 – 1970)
#1234

One of Francie doll's greatest outfits! This multiple piece/multiple look ensemble started off with a green knit sleeveless shell and a paisley tricot blouse. Either top was great with the blue velveteen skirt with yoke and an attached golden chain belt. A cuddly white faux caracul coat was lined in paisley and piped in velveteen. A matching faux caracul hat with green knit band, green knit stockings, and go-go boots completed the ensemble. $300.00

Skipper Doll Ensemble Paks for 1969

Skipper doll had twelve new Ensemble Paks plus a Sears exclusive for 1969.

Twist 'n Turn
Skipper Doll
Original Outfit (1969)
#1105

Bright for the beach! The red and orange checked suit featured solid orange trim. $45.00

Jeepers Creepers (1969 – 1970)
#1966

Skipper doll was dressed for a day of play outdoors. Bright red and soft blue combined in a polka dot top and pair of striped pedal pushers. Each piece featured solid blue trim. A red, plastic sun visor with a blue scarf, blue flats, sunglasses, and a red and blue ball completed the playful look. $150.00

Jazzy 'Jamas (1969 – 1970)
#1967

Cute baby dolls in peachy pink sheer nylon lined in orange nylon featured a puffed sleeve top with a ruffle at the hem with a white string bow accent. Lace trimmed the puffed sleeves and the matching panties. White felt slippers featured nylon squares on top. $150.00

Hopscotchins (1969 – 1970)
#1968

Skipper doll's cute green Bermudas featured patch pockets and a pink and yellow plastic belt held by two, yellow vinyl belt loops. The rainbow striped long sleeved shirt had three golden bead buttons. A pair of blue flats completed the ensemble. $125.00

Knit Bit (1969 – 1970)
#1969

This cute crocheted-look knit set was bright in hot pink. The sleeveless tunic featured two blue shank buttons at the neckline and a blue crocheted belt. Matching shorts, a crocheted blue and hot pink headband, hot pink nylon knee socks, and go-go boots completed the playful set. $150.00

Ice Cream 'n Cake (1969 – 1970)
#1970

A party perfect look featured a dressy shirt dress with long sleeved lace trimmed bodice with three blue buttons. The blue textured skirt featured a front pleat. A contrasting pink vinyl belt, matching lace trimmed panties, white cotton lace hose, and white flats completed the party fun ensemble. $200.00

Pants 'n Pinafore (1969 – 1970)
#1971

A very versatile outfit for casual days or those dressy occasions. The red-orange pants dress featured long sleeves and a yellow vinyl waistband. Two golden bead buttons accented the side of the waistband and there was one on each sleeve. A cute ruffled scarf tied under the chin. For a more dressy look, Skipper doll did not wear the hat, but wore a white-on-white striped pinafore which changed the look entirely. Red-orange flats looked great with either look. $200.00

Drizzle Sizzle (1969 – 1970)
#1972

This has to be the wildest outfit Skipper doll ever wore in the rain! Her long sleeved knit dress was hot pink and chartreuse with flower cut-outs as trim. The clear plastic raincoat featured red-orange trim and front closures. There was a matching hood and clear plastic boots with painted trim. $225.00

Chilly Chums (1969 – 1970)
#1973

Skipper doll chose this great outfit for a chilly Easter Sunday. The pink and yellow floral dress featured a roll collar, ruffled front, and dropped waist. A solid pink coat had six golden bead buttons at the double-breasted closure and one at each sleeve tab. A self belt featured a square buckle. A pink tie on bonnet, pink sheer nylon hose, and yellow flats completed the perky set. $225.00

Eeny, Meeny, Midi (1969 – 1970)
#1974

Ruffles, ribbons, and lace created this frothy sunshine yellow party dress. The white lace dress featured puffed sleeves and three rows of double ruffles on the midi skirt. Bright yellow lined the dress and a yellow bow accented the empire waist. Yellow tricot pettipants were trimmed in lace. Yellow flats, a hot pink package with yellow ribbon and flower accent and a cardboard face mirror with metallic paper "mirror" completed the set. $225.00

Sunny Suity (1969 – 1970)
#1975

An adorable sunsuit for days of summer fun!
A yellow textured lightweight knit formed the
sleeveless pants dress with empire waist.
White lace accented either side of the
bodice and the matching dust cap. A hot
pink satin waistband with bow added accent
color contrast to the suit. Novelty soft vinyl
sandals featured cut-outs and a golden bead
button side closure. $225.00

School's Cool (1969 – 1970)
#1976

A smock-styled dress featured a bright modern art floral print. The dress had a sheer dotted Swiss collar and
puffed sleeves. A big patch pocket had a gathered top.
Bright melon opaque tricot tights, pink go go boots and
a pink princess telephone completed the artistic ensemble. $200.00

Plaid City (1969 – 1970)
#1977

A wonderful suit look for Skipper doll in chartreuse, turquoise, and white. The chartreuse
pleated skirt was topped by a button front top
trimmed with turquoise knit and the three buttons. A turquoise knit dickie accented the neckline. For a chilly day, a big checked jacket
featured six turquoise buttons and a knit collar
that matched the knit tam. Chartreuse flats
completed the look. $225.00

Sears Exclusive
Bright 'n Breezy Set
Skipper Doll Gift Set (1969)
#1590

The pretty Twist 'n Turn Skipper doll had a cute blue romper with green braid and vinyl trim. A green vinyl coat featured blue faux fur collar and cuffs. Green flats completed the winning look. This set is also known as Wow! What A Cool Outfit, as it is called in the Sears catalog. $2,000.00

Tutti Doll Ensemble Paks for 1969

Tutti doll had no new ensembles for 1969 but her four fashions from 1968 were repeated. These were Sea-Shore Shorties #3614, Flower Girl #3615, Pink P.J.s #3616, and Birthday Beauties #3617.

Chapter III — 1970

A Year of Action

This year featured a new level of articulation in the beautiful Living Barbie and Skipper dolls who could pose in a more realistic way. 1970 also saw the addition of a new friend for Ken doll and a boyfriend for Christie doll in the new Brad doll. The beautiful new Walking Jamie from Sears was introduced and the adorable Pretty Pairs were added.

The costumes still maintained a high quality standard. Barbie doll had 31 outfits in the Ensemble Pak line, six new paks, and seven store exclusives. There were 18 costumes and one gift set repeated from 1969. The repeats were Winter Wedding #1880, Salute To Silver package, Dream Wrap #1476, Hurray For Leather #1477, Shift Into Knit #1478, Leisure Leopard #1479, Firelights #1481, Important In-Vestment #1482, Little Bow Pink #1483, Yellow-Mellow #1484, Winter Wow #1486, Shirtdressy #1487, Velvet Venture #1488, Cloud 9 #1489, Red, White 'n Warm #1491, Silver Polish #1492, Fab Fur #1493, Goldswinger #1494. The gift set repeated was the J. C. Penney Talking Barbie Doll Pink Premiere Set #1596. Julia doll's four outfits were also repeated. These were Leather Weather #1751, Brr-Furr #1752, Candlelight Capers #1753, and Pink Fantasy #1754.

Original Outfits for the Barbie Size Dolls from 1970

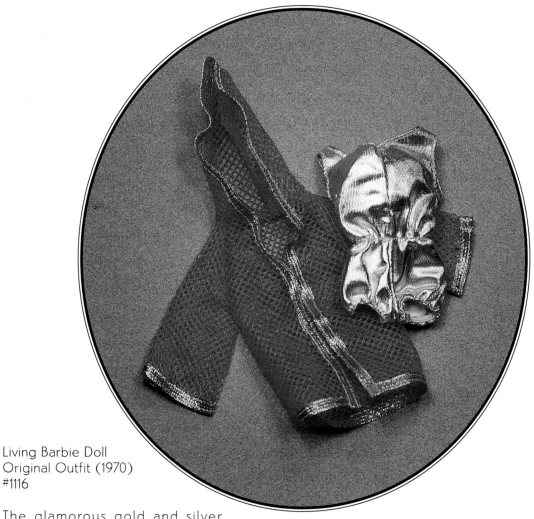

Living Barbie Doll
Original Outfit (1970)
#1116

The glamorous gold and silver
metallic knit swimsuit was accented with a bright orange nylon net hooded
cover-up with golden braid trim. $45.00

Living Barbie Doll From Japan
Original Outfit (1970)
#11168

The Japanese issue of the Living Barbie doll was the same doll in pink leotard and tights as the one in the Sears Exclusive Action Accents gift set #1585 from 1970 – 1971. $100.00

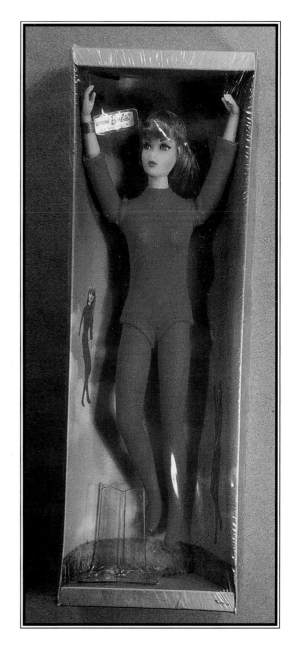

Living Eli Doll From Japan
Original Outfit (1970)

Barbie doll's friend from Japan wore a similar outfit to that of Living Barbie doll's from Japan. Eli doll's was bright red instead of pink. $150.00

Sears Exclusive
Walking Jamie Doll
Original Outfit (1970 – 1972)
#1132

The beautiful doll wore a bright mini dress with block design, belt, and rolled collar. A nylon scarf, panties, and orange boots completed the outfit. $100.00

Twist 'n Turn Barbie Doll
Original Outfit (1970)
#1160

This year, the suit featured a graphic floral design in rose and white, or hot pink and white tricot. $50.00

Twist 'n Turn Stacey Doll
Original Outfit (1970 – 1971)
#1125

Stacey doll's hard-to-find swimsuit was a bright blue and pink floral print on tricot. It featured simple, one-piece styling. $75.00

Twist 'n Turn P.J. Doll
Original Outfit (1970 – 1971)
#1118

Her modest one-piece swimsuit was fashioned from pink tricot with a crocheted-look skirt and orange vinyl belt. $50.00

Standard Barbie Doll
Original Outfit (1970 – 1971)
#1190

The nicely detailed suit featured green and pink tricot with split shoulder straps and floral accent. $50.00

Twist 'n Turn
Christie Doll
Original Outfit (1970 – 1971)
#1119

The doll's tricot suit featured pink, yellow and white in a geometric print with solid color top. $75.00

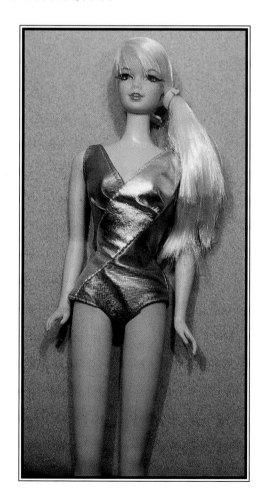

Talking Stacey Doll
Original Outfit (1970 – 1971)
#1125

This wonderful doll wore a silver and blue metallic knit one-piece swimsuit. $50.00

Talking Christie Doll
Original Outfit (1970 – 1971)
#1126

The new look had a wonderful, African inspired flavor in the print top with orange leather-look vinyl trim with matching vinyl panties. $50.00

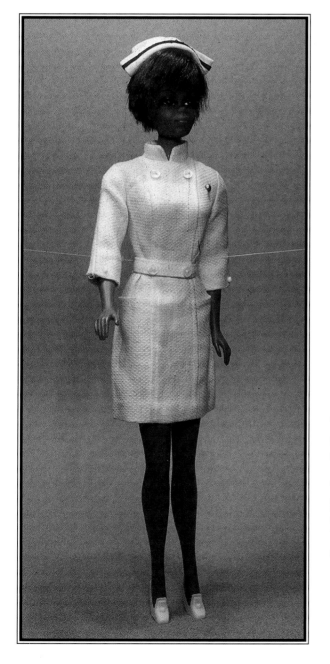

Twist 'n Turn Julia Doll
Original Outfit (1970 – 1971)
#1127

This year, Julia doll's uniform featured one-piece double-breasted styling. The waistline sported a button trimmed waistband and her nurse's pin was attached to the bodice. The nurse's cap had black braid trim and she wore white chunky shoes. $75.00

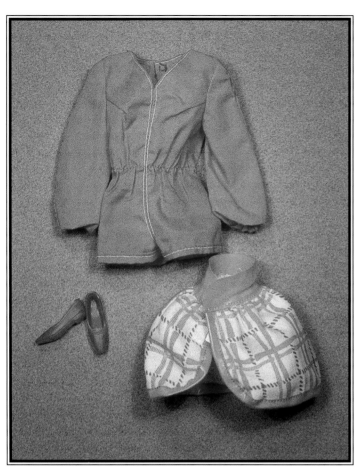

Tangerine Scene (1970)
#1451

A cute, long sleeved tangerine body suit was topped by a plaid wrap mini. The skirt was trimmed in tangerine vinyl. Orange flats completed the set. $175.00

Now Knit (1970)
#1452

This sharp combination in lime and navy knit was accented by "silver." The sleeveless sheath dress featured the three colors in horizontal bands. Also, a silvertone wide plastic belt and a lime plush hat featured a navy tricot lining and hatband. A navy tricot scarf with silvertone slide closure and navy chunky shoes completed the look. $175.00

Flower Wower (1970)
#1453

Beautiful soft pastels colored this bold floral print tent dress in sheer cotton. The empire style dress featured long bell sleeves and a rosette at the V neck. Chartreuse chunky shoes completed Barbie doll's summery set. $175.00

Loop Scoop (1970)
#1454

Heavy yellow cotton created this sleeveless dress which featured a skirt of colorful rows of braid below the dropped waist. The dress had built-in panties. Yellow chunky shoes added the perfect color accent. $150.00

Dreamy Blues (1970)
#1456

Barbie doll looked like a dream in her blue satin mini dress with light and medium blue and yellow ruffled organza skirt. The waist was accented with a blue velvet ribbon waistband and rosette. Blue chunky shoes completed the feminine look. $150.00

City Sparkler (1970)
#1457

This pretty non-pink party dress featured a green lamé shirt dress bodice with contrasting chartreuse chiffon skirt. Two pearl-look buttons accented the placket front. Chartreuse chunky shoes completed this unusual dress in Barbie doll's wardrobe. $175.00

Gypsy Spirit (1970)
#1458

Barbie doll's pink tricot body blouse featured golden braid at the neck and the cuffs. Turquoise velveteen fashioned the mini skirt and vest. Each of these pieces was trimmed with a pink and chartreuse loop braid and the golden braid as well. Hot pink chunky shoes completed the ensemble. $175.00

Great Coat (1970)
#1459

Barbie doll stepped out in style in her yellow vinyl coat trimmed in faux leopard. Her matching vinyl hat also had "leopard" trim. Yellow chunky shoes completed the set. $175.00

Rare Pair (1970)
#1462

Bright yellow and hot pink knit formed this mod jacket dress. The sleeveless dress featured an empire waist, two pleats in the A-line skirt, and four golden bead buttons at the top of the pleats. The jacket also featured the two-color combination. Yellow nylon hose and chunky shoes completed the set. $175.00

Lovely Sleep-Ins (1970)
#1463

Beautiful pink nylon formed the ¾ length gown with ruffled hem and empire tucked bodice. The gown was lined with tricot. The pink robe was fashioned from a sheer, floral printed nylon lace. A furry collar and cuffs and a tie at the neck plus a pair of furry slippers added the finishing touch. $175.00

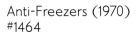

Anti-Freezers (1970)
#1464

A sleeveless, yellow cotton shell was topped by a red, white, and yellow plaid knit mini. A red knit coat featured five golden bead buttons and a crocheted tie belt. A plaid scarf and yellow vinyl boots completed the chill chasing outfit! $175.00

Lemon Kick (1970)
#1465

This beautiful and versatile ensemble was fashioned from lemon mini-pleated nylon. The long sleeved dress/top worked well as a top with the palazzo pants or as a mini dress with the nylon underpants included. The empire waist was defined by white floral braid and a contrasting hot pink nylon bow. Yellow chunky shoes completed the ensemble. $200.00

Lamb 'n Leather (1970)
#1467

Barbie doll's fashionable coat was created from a lamb's-wool-look faux fur lined in pink silk. The mini style was accented by black vinyl trimmed patch pockets, a black and pink vinyl belt with single golden bead button closure. Boots carried out the theme in pink with black accents as did the circular handbag. The look was topped off with a lamb's-wool-look hat with pom pon. $250.00

Special Sparkle (1970)
#1468

This three-piece evening ensemble featured a hot pink shell and a golden jersey skirt. The skirt had a braid waistband with pink loops and golden chains. The opulent fitted coat was fashioned from a hot pink and gold lamé and was lined in hot pink nylon. The golden knit fabric formed the lapels. An attached wide golden braid belt with circular textured buckle, hot pink stockings and chunky shoes accented the set. $250.00

Blue Royalty (1970)
#1469

The changeable shiny turquoise evening gown featured an empire waist bodice and full flared skirt with pleat. Metallic braid accented the bodice and a goldtone and iridescent border of braid trimmed the skirt. A pretty, white faux fur bolero was trimmed with golden braid and lined in turquoise satin. Turquoise chunky shoes completed the elegant ensemble. $250.00

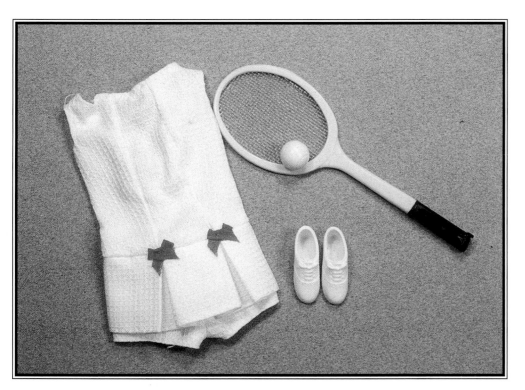

Tennis Team (1970 – 1971)
#1781

Barbie doll was ready for the courts in her perky piqué tennis dress with pleated front and red accent bows. Matching panties, tennis shoes, plastic ball, and racquet completed the winning set. $150.00

Shape-Ups (1970 – 1971)
#1782

Now we know how Barbie doll keeps her perfect figure! This shapely exercise set featured a red, long sleeved jersey leotard, sheer red tights, and red buckle flats. Barbie doll's exercise equipment consisted of two black plastic hand weights, a twist exerciser, an elastic pull, and a How To booklet written by Living Barbie doll herself, of course! $175.00

Ruffles 'n Swirls (1970 – 1971)
#1783

This bright and feminine dress was perfect for a hot summer day. The lightweight turquoise fabric was swirled with hot pink. A pink plastic belt completed the ruffled dress. Fuchsia chunky shoes completed the set. (Also shown is a harder to find variation in a pink floral print. The fabric is a much heavier weight and has a slight woven stripe texture.) $175.00

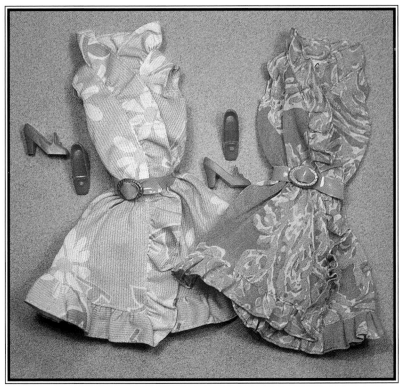

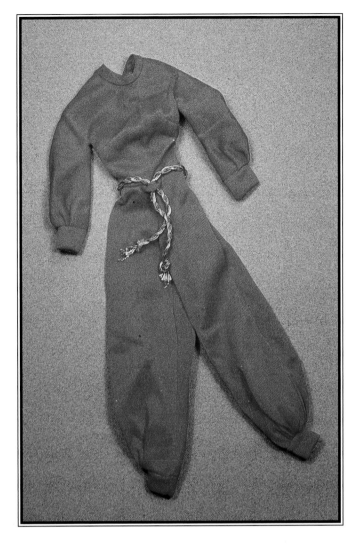

Harem-m-m's (1970 – 1971)
#1784

Looking like she just popped out of a genie's bottle, Barbie doll wore a one-piece harem pants style jumpsuit. The sleeves and the pants legs were full and gathered into cuffs. Her tiny waist was accented by a gold and silvertone woven tie belt. $150.00

Bright 'n Brocade (1970 – 1971)
#1786

A beautiful lamé brocade fabric was the highlight of this pantsuit. The pinks, metallic golds, and a bit of emerald were woven into an interesting wrapped and fitted long sleeved blouse. Hot pink sheer pants were trimmed with the blouse fabric. Pink bow shoes completed the set. $225.00

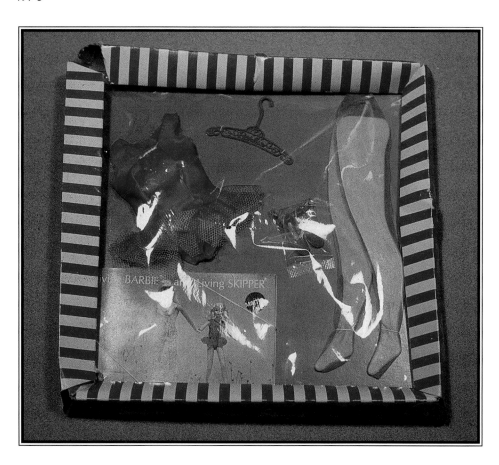

Prima Ballerina (1970 – 1971)
#1787

The brightest ballet tutu in Barbie doll's wardrobe. An almost day-glow hot pink satin fabric formed the body of the tutu. Multiple layers of tulle in yellow, orange, and hot pink formed the skirt. Hot pink sheer pantyhose and hot pink ballet slippers with ties completed the ensemble. $225.00

Scuba-do's (1970 – 1971)
#1788

Ready for some scuba diving, Barbie doll wore a multicolor print two-piece swimsuit. This was topped by a yellow, fleecy hooded cover-up. Bright orange plastic swim fins, face mask with clear inset, and a snorkel completed the set. $175.00

Fiery Felt (1970 – 1971)
#1789

Warm fabric, hot color! This bright red-orange felt coat featured a double row of fringe at the hem and five golden bead buttons. The felt hat featured fringe trim. Red mid-calf boots completed the winter look. $150.00

The Lace Caper (1970 – 1971)
#1791

Beautiful white diamond lace formed the flared leg slacks topped with a matching long sleeved tunic. The body of the tunic was lined with tricot and the neckline featured a floral braid. A long, hot pink nylon cape featured a tie at the neck. Hot pink chunky shoes completed the beautiful hostess ensemble. $200.00

Mood Matchers (1970 – 1971)
#1792

A colorful jersey print formed a cute mini dress with turquoise jersey waist inset and accent bow. The great palazzo pants teamed with a long sleeved turquoise jersey blouse. A turquoise vinyl belt with oval buckle and chunky shoes completed the set. $200.00

Skate Mates (1970 – 1971)
#1793

Guaranteed to be the most attention-getting costume on the ice, Barbie doll's bright red velveteen skating dress sported white, curly faux fur sleeves and trim at the hem. She wore a matching cap with furry trim. Her mittens were red with furry tops. Bright red sheer pantyhose with an opaque tricot panty and white ice skates with silver plastic blades completed Barbie doll's look. $200.00

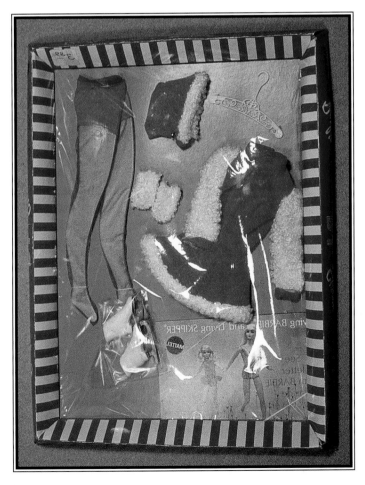

Check The Suit (1970 – 1971)
#1794

Stylish and warm! This oversize houndstooth fabric was electric in yellow and hot pink. The slacks sported an attached yellow vinyl belt with golden buckle and were topped by a short jacket with yellow knit collar and four large hot pink buttons on the double breasted front. A yellow knit shell and chunky shoes completed the wintery ensemble. $175.00

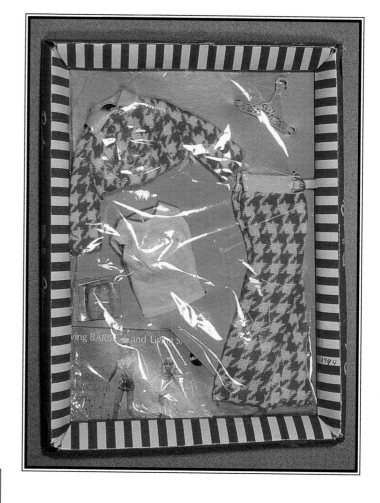

Fur Sighted (1970)
#1796

Barbie doll's red pantsuit featured an interestingly textured fabric and real fur trim. The slacks were topped by a red, yellow, and metallic silver knit shell. The jacket featured three golden plastic frogs at bead button closures. Two rows of yellow fur fringe were edged with golden braid. A red cap with golden neck strap and fur trim plus yellow chunky shoes accessorized the set. (Color variations are shown with one being very orange and the other, very red!) $225.00

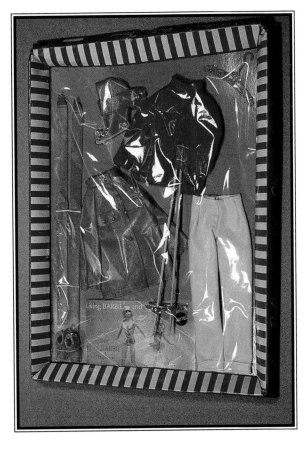

Rainbow Wraps (1970)
#1798

An oversize geometric print swirled on the satin in rose, red-orange, green, blue and white outlined in black. The full skirt dress featured a metallic green knit bodice with straps. A big, bright red-orange satin ribbon bow accented the waistband of the same ribbon. Barbie doll had a matching triangular shawl with red-orange fringe. A long pink nylon sheer slip with ruffle and white flower and bow accent was included. Blue chunky shoes accented the sophisticated evening ensemble. $275.00

The Ski Scene (1970)
#1797

Tri-color separates added excitement to the slopes. Barbie doll wore yellow vinyl pants with a big purple-pink long sleeved sweater and a red-orange vinyl jacket with raglan sleeves and flaps at the yoke. Two golden bead buttons trimmed each flap and three buttoned the front. A matching red-orange vinyl hood with single bead button closure and gray lining, goggles of red vinyl with clear lenses wrapped around the head and also fastened with a single golden bead button. Red-orange plastic skis, poles, and ski boots completed the snow set. $250.00

Maxi 'n Midi (1970)
#1799

This has to be one of Barbie doll's wildest outfits of all time! A multicolor stripe knit woven with metallic thread was fashioned into a sleeveless sheath with golden metallic thin tie belt. The mod maxi coat was fashioned of a very shiny blue metallic fabric with matching furry trim on the collar and accenting the hem. A self belt with buckle cinched in the waist. Super tall hip boots were designed in metallic blue jersey. $300.00

Barbie Doll Fashion Paks for 1970

There were six new fashion paks for Barbie doll and her friends in 1970. They contained accessories, costume completers, dressmaker details and total outfits!

Stitch 'n Style (1970)
#0010

This pak of dress maker details featured two zippers; a package each of belt buckles, golden bead buttons, silvery bead buttons, pink shank buttons with "diamond" sets, and separate packs of red and turquoise shank buttons; blue, pink, and yellow flat buttons; pink "pearl" and pink flowers with yellow bead centers. Shown are variations in zipper colors. $75.00

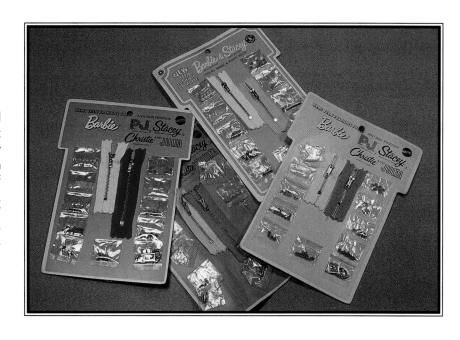

Sharp Shift (1970)
#0020

This pretty, long sleeved shift was fashioned of knit fabric. Chunky shoes completed the pak. Shown are several variations. $75.00

Cool Casuals (1970)
#0030

Bright summer go-togethers; wide leg pants with matching halter were teamed with matching chunky shoes. Shown are variations. $75.00

Foot Lights (1970)
#0040

Eight pairs of shoes and three pairs of boots filled out Barbie doll's shoe wardrobe! They were white rain boots; gray and red-orange go-go boots; red, chartreuse, yellow, black, purple, fuchsia flats; and two pairs of turquoise chunky shoes. $75.00

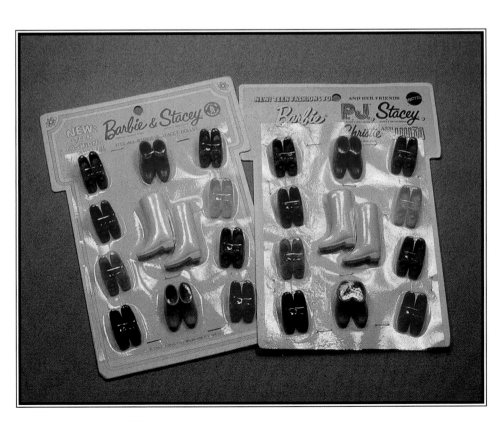

All The Trimmings! (1970)
#0050

Pretty accessories! Pink nylon fishnet hose; orange plastic rectangular drop earrings; a golden chain belt with a circular drop; golden short knit gloves; pink satin purse with golden accents and chain; braid hairpiece with brass barrette and pink ribbon. $75.00

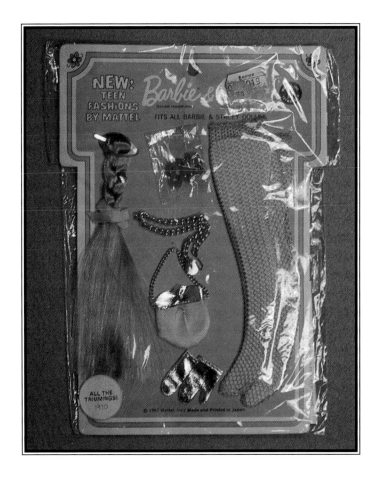

Perfect Beginnings (1970)
#0060

Pretty bra and panties with coordinating sheer petticoat with ruffle. Accessory was a golden box of talc with puff. This set came in several variations which are shown. $75.00

Department Store Exclusive Fashions and Gift Sets for 1970

There were five accessory and fashion paks and two gift sets from Sears and J. C. Penney for 1970.

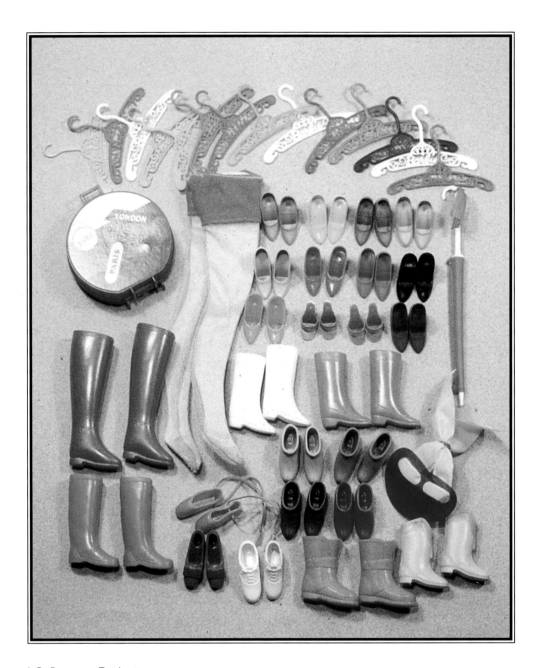

J.C. Penney Exclusive
Shoe Bag 64-Piece
Accessory Set 1970 – 1971
#1498

The extensive set included closed toe pumps in light green or chartreuse, yellow, purple, hot pink, aqua, royal, orange, and black;. two pairs of hot pink open toe shoes; tall cerise boots; blue rain boots; white boots with heels; hot pink galoshes; pale blue majorette boots with painted chartreuse trim; and gray, red, blue, and green go-go boots. Also included were white tennis shoes, hot pink ballet slippers, and blue bow shoes. Other accessories included pink pantyhose with net panty and golden bow (see Pink Premiere gift set #1596 for hose); sun visor; hat box; hangers; and umbrella. $200.00

Sears Exclusive
Glamour Group (1970 – 1971)
#1510

The set consisted of a casual knit dress with vinyl belt and clutch, cotton dress with rickrack, dressy dress, faux fur trimmed coat, nightie and panties, pantyhose and shoes. Fabric variations are shown. $150.00

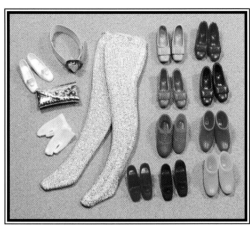

Sears Exclusive
Fashion Accents
(1970 – 1974)
#1521

The pak contained bow shoes in dark blue, pale blue, orange, and red; chunky shoes in red, white, and blue; go-go boots in orange and yellow; turquoise tennis shoes; short white gloves; silvertone clutch bag; silvertone belt and silver knit stockings. $100.00

Sears Exclusive
Fashion Bouquet (1970 – 1973)
#1511

A four-piece suit consisted of blouse, jacket, skirt, and pants. Also included were a coat, two-piece swimsuit, daytime dress, plus shoes, scarf, and sunglasses. $150.00

Shown at left are variations in the fabrics of pieces in Fashion Bouquet #1511.

Sears Exclusive
Goodies Galore (1970 – 1973)
#1518

Lots of fun time accessories included red molded vinyl cap; short white gloves; tennis racquet and ball; sundae; transistor radio; yellow and white chunky shoes; purple, blue, and pink cut-out shoes; green, blue, yellow, and red square toe shoes; ice skates; pale pink ballet slippers; brown laced front boots; pink and red sunglasses; red-orange vinyl handbag; seven hangers; white with red knit hat with pom pon; comb, brush, and curlers in later sets. $150.00

Sears Exclusive
Living Barbie
Action Accents Gift Set (1970 – 1971)
#1585

The beautiful Living Barbie doll (the version made in Japan found only in this set in the U.S, but sold separately in Japan) was dressed in a hot pink leotard and tights for a workout with her exercise cord. She could add to this basic outfit and create other active looks. There was a hot pink and orange vinyl ski jacket with skis, ski poles, and boots. For ice skating, she added the pink faux fur trimmed blue velveteen skating skirt, furry bonnet, and blue ice skates. For ballet, she tied on her orange and hot pink tulle tutu and added her ballet slippers. For snorkeling, she wore a blue and orange swimsuit with floral accent with swim fins, mask, and snorkel. $1,500.00

Sears Exclusive
Mad About Plaid
Gift Set (1970)
#1587

Talking Barbie doll was featured in this set that included a huge, red plaid mini dress with green vinyl belt and a matching plaid coat. A red furry hat, plaid clutch bag with green vinyl flap and golden bead button, and chunky shoes completed the ensemble. $1,200.00

Sears Exclusive
P.J. Doll
Swingin' In Silver (1970)
#1588

Twist 'n Turn P.J. doll had a glamorous evening ensemble all her own! The dress had a pink satin bodice with nylon jabot with one silvertone bead button and silver knit skirt. The silver knit coat and boots had white faux fur trim. $1,500.00

Sears Exclusive
Jamie Doll
Furry Friends Gift Set (1970 – 1971)
#1584

This pretty Sears exclusive doll wore the original outfit that the doll wore when sold separately. This was a block print knit dress with attached elastic belt, head scarf, and orange boots. The gift set also included an orange furry coat with knit sleeves and hat with pink vinyl trim and pink chunky shoes. A cute gray poodle with pink vinyl collar and leash, dog food box, yellow dog food bowl, and bone completed the set. $1,500.00

Ken Doll's Looks in 1970

Talking Ken Doll (1970)
#1111

He wore a new, two-piece suit with orange trunks and blue and orange beach jacket. $40.00

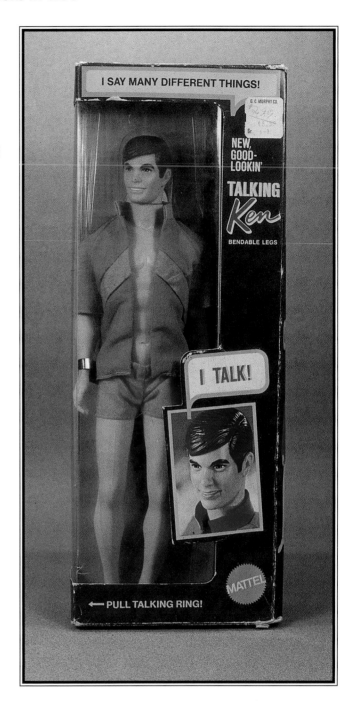

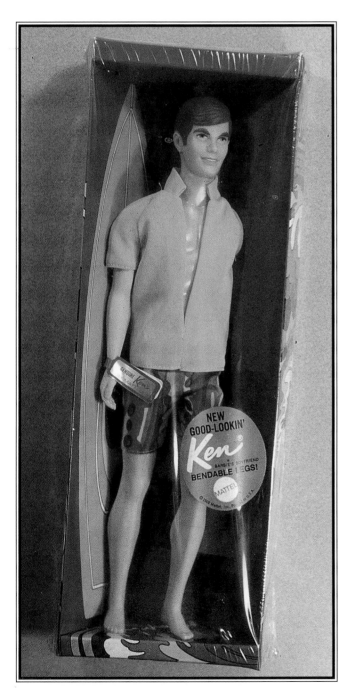

Bendable Leg Ken Doll
Original Outfit (1970 – 1971)
#1124

His open front, ochre tricot shirt topped mod print cotton trunks. $50.00

Bendable Leg Brad Doll (1970 – 1972)
#1142

His bright red tricot shirt topped coordinating printed cotton trunks. $50.00

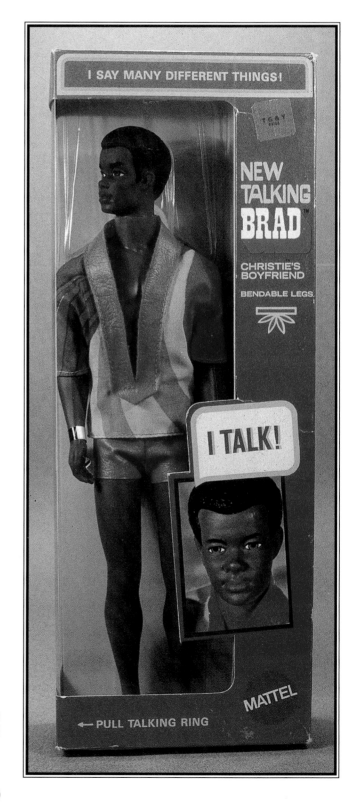

Talking Brad Doll
Original Outfit (1970 – 1973)
#1114

Brad doll's outfit featured a bright print shirt with orange leather-look vinyl trim and trunks. His outfit coordinated with Talking Christie doll's outfit #1126. $50.00

Ensemble Pak Assortment for Ken Doll in 1970

Four Ensemble Paks for Ken and Brad dolls were available in 1970. Although the number of outfits was limited, Ken doll had a dressy suit, a swim and sports outfit, a casual suit, and a winter outfit with warm double breasted coat. Four outfits were repeated. These were Breakfast At 7 #1428, Rally Gear #1429, Town Turtle #1430, and Guruvy Formal #1431. And, a Sears exclusive outfit and gift set were also available.

Play It Cool (1970)
#1433

For those chilly winter days, Ken doll wore a red turtleneck with zippered slacks fashioned from an oversized plaid knit fabric in tan, red, and black. He topped off his look with a tan felt double-breasted coat with four buttons and pocket flaps. Brown shoes and red socks completed his look. $175.00

Big Business (1970)
#1434

Ken doll's traditional suit featured updated styling. The black tiny houndstooth suit had wide lapels, side vents, and double-breasted styling. His accessories were truly mod—his bright blue short sleeved shirt coordinated with a bright tie. Black socks and shoes completed his look. $200.00

Shore Lines (1970)
#1435

Ken doll's flashy sporting outfit prepared him for land or sea. On land, Ken doll wore a bright blue long raglan sleeved jacket with yellow zip front. His slacks were an incredibly wild geometric print in vivid blue, yellow, red, green, and orange. For snorkeling, Ken doll had a pair of blue trunks with drawstring waist and orange and yellow side stripes. Yellow swim fins, snorkel, and face mask with clear plastic window completed the outfit. $200.00

Bold Gold (1970)
#1436

This casual suit look featured textured gold zippered slacks, yellow jersey mock turtle and a lightweight plaid jacket in gold, cream, and burgundy plaid. Completing the look were gold socks and brown shoes. $200.00

Sears Exclusive Outfit
Casual All Stars (1970)
#1514

His mix and matchables were two pairs of slacks, two shirts, a jacket,
swim trunks, socks, shoes, and two ties. $125.00

Sears Exclusive
Red, White And Wild Set (1970)
#1589

Handsome bendable Ken doll's gift set included red slacks with a blue short sleeved tricot shirt and a loud red, white, and blue double-breasted jacket. A yellow polka dotted tie, blue socks, and navy shoes completed the set. $1,500.00

Francie Doll Ensemble Paks from 1970

Francie doll's wardrobe for 1970 featured sixteen new styles for Francie and Casey dolls to share in the Ensemble Pak line. Eight styles were also repeated. These were Something Else #1219, Land Ho #1220, Tennis Tunic #1221, Gold Rush #1222, Pink Lightning #1231, Two For The Ball #1232, Victorian Wedding #1233, and The Combination #1234. An exclusive Sears outfit was also available this year.

Twist 'n Turn Francie Doll
Original Outfit (1970)
#1170

The bold floral print was fashioned into a lace trimmed wrap style with accent bow and shoulder straps of braid. A pink vinyl panty completed the look. $50.00

Hair Happenin's Francie Doll
Original Outfit (1970 – 1972)
#1122

The pretty teen doll wore a blue tricot dress with built-in panty and white crocheted-look trim, a ribbon headband, and pumps. $45.00

Francie Doll With Growing Pretty Hair
Original Outfit (1970 – 1973)
#1129

The pink party dress featured a metallic knit empire bodice and lacy overskirt with pink nylon lining. Braid accented the waist. Pink pumps completed the look. $45.00

Satin Happenin' (1970 – 1971, 1974)
#1237

This elegant jumpsuit ensemble featured a rose satin that had an almost dayglo quality to it. The simple strapless style had wide legs and was topped by a small floral pattern lace top. The ¾ sleeves and hem were trimmed with the satin which also formed the accessorizing bow at the neck. Hot pink square toe shoes completed the ensemble. $200.00

Snappy Snoozers (1970 – 1971, 1974)
#1238

This cute mini sleep ensemble enveloped Francie or Casey doll in a flurry of hot pink ruffles! The short peignoir was fashioned from sheer nylon and accented with row after row of ruffles on the entire garment, including the sleeves. This topped a simple tricot gown with empire waist and two ruffles at the hem. White felt slippers with hot pink accents completed the look. $150.00

Bloom Zoom (1970 – 1971, 1974)
#1239

This adorable mod mini ensemble featured a bright floral print on jersey. The tights and the long sleeved, empire waist dress were fashioned from the floral fabric. A blue vinyl vest was flocked in orange on the outside. Two blue shank buttons trimmed the closure. Blue buckle flats completed the ensemble. $200.00

Pony Coat (1970 – 1971, 1974)
#1240

This warm fake fur coat featured a dark brown on cream spotted print. The collar, pocket tabs, and wide belt were fashioned from white textured vinyl. The coat was lined with contrasting green satin and white pumps were included. $200.00

Altogether Elegant (1970 – 1971, 1974)
#1242

Youthful elegance was the hallmark of Francie doll's two-piece evening ensemble. The dress and short jacket duo featured white printed sheer "lace" with the hottest pink satin lining. The dress was sleeveless with a hem ruffle and a metallic silvertone braid band at the empire waist and neckline. The jacket featured braid on the bell sleeves and three silvertone bead buttons accented the snap front. A silvertone clutch bag, short white gloves, and hot pink square toe shoes completed the ensemble. $250.00

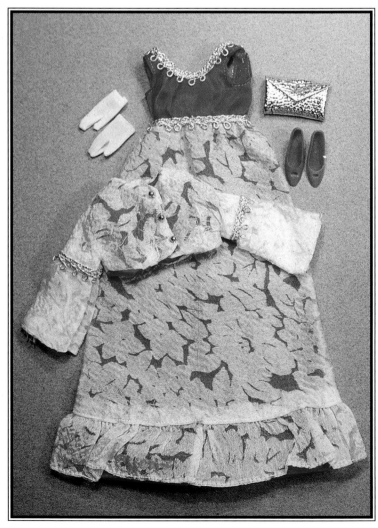

Striped Types (1970 – 1971, 1974)
#1243

Only Francie, Casey and Twiggy dolls could look so good in horizontal stripes! The red and navy three-piece knit set featured a turtleneck with a navy collar and body, and long red sleeves and yoke. The slightly bell bottomed pants and long vest were made of the striped knit. Four golden buttons and vinyl pocket tabs accented the vest. Dark blue buckle flats completed the casual outfit. $175.00

Wedding Whirl (1970 – 1971, 1974)
#1244

Francie doll enjoyed modelling this lovely bridal gown. The sheer fabric featured a scalloped white-on-white design at the hems of the full skirt and bell sleeves. It was lined with satin and featured pale pink satin ribbon at the empire waist and on the sleeves. A lacy braid trim accented the neckline and formed the head-piece for the tulle veil. White closed toe pumps and a bouquet of three white satin flowers on tulle with a transparent green-plastic, scalloped base tied with grosgrain ribbon completed the ensemble. $275.00

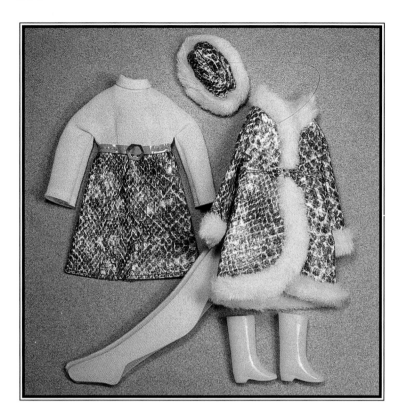

Snake Charmers (1970 – 1971, 1974)
#1245

A wonderful quality faux snakeskin was fashioned into this stylish coat and dress for Francie doll. The dress featured a yellow bodice with long sleeves and roll neck, A-line "snakeskin" mini skirt and an orange vinyl belt at the empire waist. The "snakeskin" A-line coat featured yellow fake fur trim around the neck, front, sleeves and hem. The cute "snakeskin" hat also was trimmed in the "fur." Yellow pantyhose and mid-calf boots completed the ensemble. $250.00

Sears Exclusive Outfit
Pretty Power (1970 – 1973)
#1512

Francie doll's cute coordinates included a knit shirt; vest and skirt with a viny waistband; floral nightie and panties; dressy dress with a wide golden belt with buckle; petticoat; vinyl coat with belt; pantyhose; stockings; two pairs of shoes; and a pair of felt slippers with shank button accents. $150.00.

Sunny Slacks (1970 – 1971)
#1761

Francie doll looked cute in her bright pink body blouse with long sleeves, four silvertone buttons, and a pair of bright yellow slacks with a geometric design in orange, two shades of blue, and pink. The fabric had a woven-in vertical texture stripe. $150.00

Pink Power (1970 – 1971)
#1762

This pretty little lace mini dress featured a hot pink lacy fabric lined in tricot. A double ruffle accented the waist. Pink stockings and square toe pumps completed the lovely set. $150.00

The Entertainer (1970 – 1971)
#1763

This lovely jumpsuit was fashioned from bright melon jersey with ecru trim at the long sleeves and pants legs. A matching satin bow accented the elasticized waist. Melon square toe pumps completed the ensemble that was perfect for entertaining. $150.00

Corduroy Cape (1970 – 1971)
#1764

This cute, wide wale turquoise corduroy cape was lined in nylon and featured white or yellow faux fur at the hem. Two large golden bead buttons and a golden cord "loop" fastened under the chin. Blue boots (majorette style with front tassel) were included. $150.00

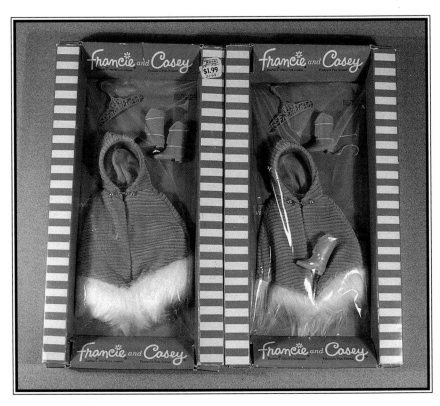

Wild Bunch (1970 – 1971)
#1766

This was an absolutely fabulous look
for Francie doll! The neon colors of
red-orange and fuchsia combined in
a little sleeveless knit dress with
mock turtleneck and crocheted tie
belt at the empire waist. She had
matching orange knit tights, orange
mid-calf boots, and golden chain
necklace. This was topped by a long-
haired faux fur coat in mingled yellow, fuchsia, and orange with orange
plastic trim at the neck, down the
front, the hem, and on the sleeves. A
knit hat with orange plastic bill fastened with a goldtone bead button.
She had short fuchsia gloves and a
black plastic camera with gray painted trim. $250.00

Plaid Plans (1970 – 1971)
#1767

Truly a product of the '70s, this pantsuit used a
huge, bright red, white, and yellow plaid knit! The
mix and match plaid pieces were slacks, a mini
skirt, and a vest with red pocket flaps. These
pieces topped a cute red knit top with six goldtone bead buttons. A plaid tam with emerald
pom pon and a long emerald crepe scarf with
added fringe added interesting contrast. Red
square toe pumps completed the ensemble.
$200.00

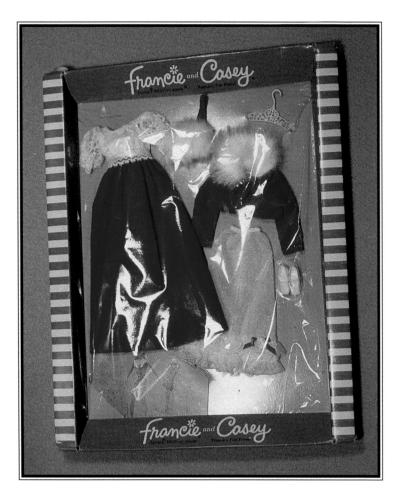

Waltz In Velvet (1970 – 1971)
#1768

This ensemble is one of Francie doll's nicest evening sets. The beautiful berry velvet dress had a white lace bodice with puffed sleeves and satin ribbon at the empire waist. A pretty short jacket featured a white faux fur collar and a furry muff with velvet back added warmth. A white, sheer nylon half slip had two double ruffles at the hem and a berry ribbon bow with yellow flower as accent. White square toe shoes completed the ensemble. $300.00

Long On Leather (1970 – 1971)
#1769

A blue, light red, and white geometric print tricot formed the simple long sleeved blouse and tights. Two pieces were fashioned from a smooth, shiny vinyl with a fabric backing. These pieces were a mini skirt with a thin vinyl belt with silvertone buckle and white top stitching and knee high boots. The long coat was fashioned from a textured vinyl with white fabric backing. It had three white shank buttons at the front and white top stitching. A long white tricot scarf with fringe added interest. $250.00

Francie Doll Fashion Paks for 1970

Francie doll had six new Fashion Paks for 1970 – 1971.

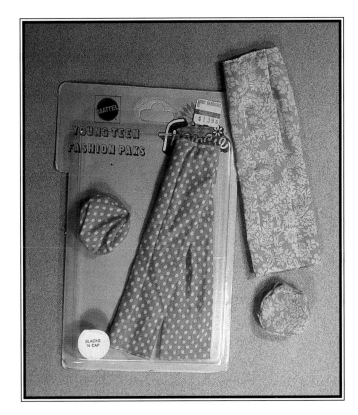

Slacks 'n Cap (1970 – 1971)

The slacks came with a coordinating cap with vinyl bill. The fabrics varied; shown are two examples. $75.00

In Step
(1970 – 1971)

Francie doll's shoe pak contained square toe pumps in white, yellow, blue, red, orange, fuchsia, and green; white tennis shoes; and palest pink ballet slippers with ties. $75.00

Super Shirt
(1970 – 1971)

This body blouse was the perfect companion for Slacks 'n Cap. Three silvertone bead buttons accented the front of the long sleeved shirt. $75.00

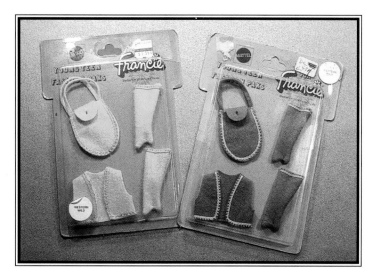

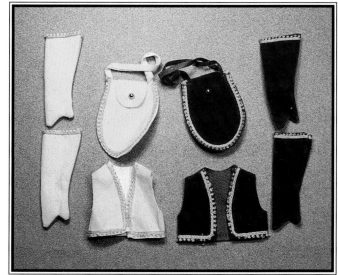

Western Wild
(1970 – 1971)

Cute Western accessories were fashioned from suedecloth. These were a vest, boots, and large bag trimmed in tiny yellow braid. Shown are color variations. $75.00

Pancho Bravo
(1970 – 1971)

The cute cover-up was fashioned from a green, fuchsia, turquoise, and white open weave fabric trimmed in white vinyl and fringe. Dark blue go-go boots and pale pink sunglasses completed the set. $75.00

Night Brights
(1970 – 1971)

This was a cute nightie for Francie doll. The fabric was bright orange tricot and the pajama top had a floral print sheer nylon overskirt. Orange bloomers and a yellow comb and brush completed the set. $75.00

Skipper Doll Ensemble Paks from 1970

Skipper doll's Ensemble Paks from 1970 featured some wonderful fabrics, colors, and ideas in the dozen new styles available. Added to this was a Sears Gift Set and an Ensemble Pak. Six new Fashion Paks were also introduced. And, the dozen Ensemble Paks introduced in 1969 were still available this year.

Re-issue
Standard Skipper Doll
Original Outfit (1970)
#0950

The same suit as the original Skipper doll wore plus accessories: red flats, comb, brush, and headband. $35.00

Twist Skipper Doll
Original Outfit (1970)
#1105

The cute Twist 'n Turn Skipper doll wore a two-piece suit that looked like three pieces. The sheer floral print top was trimmed in yellow vinyl and had an attached orange "bra" in front. The matching panty was fashioned from the orange vinyl. $50.00

Living Skipper Doll
Original Outfit (1970)
#1117

The wonderfully articulated Living Skipper doll wore a tri-color jersey swimsuit in pink, green, and blue. The color blocking extended from the bodice to the full skirt ruffle at the hip. $35.00

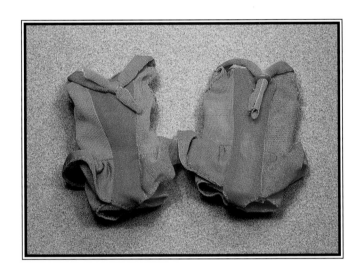

Lots of Lace (1970)
#1730

Ready for the Christmas party, Skipper doll was lovely in her green velvet, long sleeved turtleneck dress with row after row of white lace on the skirt. A lighter green ribbon with bow accented the waist. Green flats completed the set. $150.00

Budding Beauty (1970)
#1731

Another party look that would be great for a spring-time event! The sheer organdy hot fuchsia dress had long full sleeves, A-lined skirt, and white/floral print bodice with nylon lining. A contrasting chartreuse ribbon accented the empire waist. White flats completed the look. $150.00

Daisy Crazy (1970)
#1732

This was the perfect outfit for the fashion conscious sister of Barbie doll! The hot pink dress featured a big, graphic daisy print fabric for the collar, long sleeves, attached belt, and knee socks. Yellow flats completed the set. $150.00

Rik Rak Rah (1970)
#1733

The creative use of a common trim made a darling Skipper doll fun-day outfit. The dark turquoise playsuit featured yellow and white rickrack trim at the neck and the pants legs. The separate skirt of white with dark turquoise and lime stripes had yellow rickrack and yellow patent vinyl suspenders with single yellow buttons at the waist. Turquoise flats completed the look. $150.00

Twice As Nice
(1970 – 1971)
#1735

Pink and blue felt worked together for a great winter coat and dress look. The sleeveless dress featured a blue bodice meeting a pink A-line skirt at the empire waist. The coat had opposite color blocking with pink collar, yoke, sleeves, and placket above the blue body. It closed with a simple, large golden bead button. An adorable pink tam featured a pom pon made from snipped felt. Blue flats completed the set. $200.00

Super Slacks (1970 – 1971)
#1736

Skipper doll was as hip as she could be when she wore these great red and white slightly flared floral slacks with a high waist that met red vinyl suspenders with white buttons. A cute, vinyl bill cap was fashioned from the floral fabric. The white blouse had lots of lace on the front and ¾ sleeves. Red flats completed the look. $150.00

Velvet Blush (1970 – 1971)
#1737

The perfect Christmas dress would be made of red velvet trimmed in white organdy and delicate braid. That exactly describes Skipper doll's party-perfect dress with a white braid trimmed portrait collar and cuffs. White lace pantyhose and flats were perfect accessories. $200.00

Fancy Pants (1970 – 1971)
#1738

A very interesting and versatile outfit featured vinyl with floral print fabric. A hot pink vinyl bodice met three rows of the print forming the top which could be worn alone as a mini dress. The matching full pants followed the design with row after row of ruffles. A cute, hot pink vinyl purse had three yellow vinyl flowers with a white button center. Pale blue flats were included. $175.00

Wooly Winner (1970 – 1971)
#1746

What a wonderful outfit—and so perfect for a day at school! Skipper doll's dress featured a yellow knit long sleeved top with turtleneck and red/navy/yellow plaid skirt. The hat and coat featured a curly red plush trimmed in navy vinyl. A red vinyl shoulder bag, navy knit knee highs, and go-go boots completed the set. $200.00

Pink Princess (1970 – 1971)
#1747

Pink and green—what a great color combo for this coat and dress duo. The pink crepe dress was sleeveless, had an empire waist ending at a single pleat in the skirt, and featured three golden bead buttons and tiny lace trim on the bodice. The coat was whipped up in fresh green textured crepe trimmed in pink velvety ribbon and had a golden bead button at the neck and a pale pink lining. Pink pantyhose, pink faux fur hat, and white flats completed the ensemble. $200.00

Triple Treat
(1970 – 1971)
#1748

A favorite outfit featured multiple pieces in coordinating print, solid pink and warm blue velvet. The pantsuit had flared slacks with attached print waistband, a jacket with two "pearl" buttons and a bright pink knit top. The dress had the print used for the bodice, and lace trimmed the velvet skirt with a pink satin ribbon and flower to accent the empire waist. A print, three corner scarf and blue flats completed the ensemble. Shown are two variations in the print fabric used. The print looks similar but one is a lightweight voile and the other is heavier crepe. $200.00

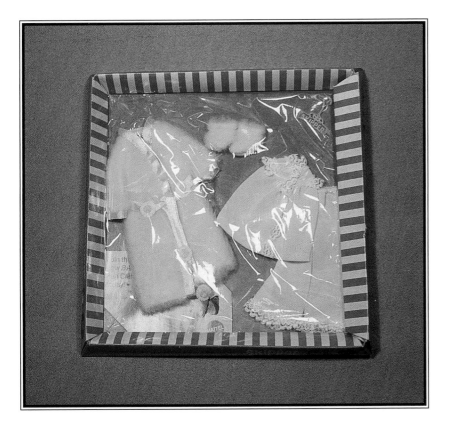

Lemon Fluff (1970 – 1971)
#1749

What little girl wouldn't like to cuddle up in this big, fluffy, long robe with satin and daisy trimmed belt? The matching pajamas featured yellow tricot and white lace trim. Skipper doll's big slippers were made from furry, fluffy plush. $200.00

Skipper Doll Fashion Paks for 1970

There were six new Fashion Paks for Skipper doll in 1970.

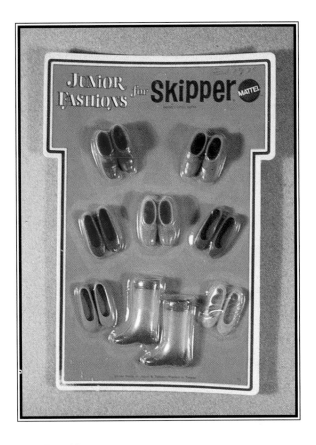

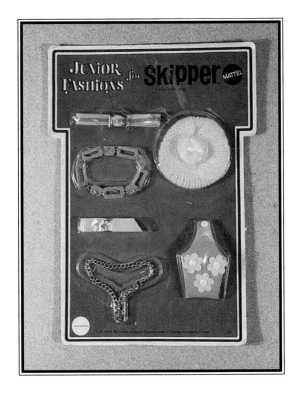

Toe Twinklers

Eight pairs of shoes and boots came together in this pak. The styles featured were clear boots with red trim; red, pink, and green go-go boots; and turquoise, red, pink, and navy flats. $75.00

Side Lights

This neat accessory pak featured a yellow knit tam with pom pon; hot pink vinyl purse with three yellow flowers; a yellow belt, a yellow/pink striped belt, a pink plastic link belt; and a golden chain belt. $75.00

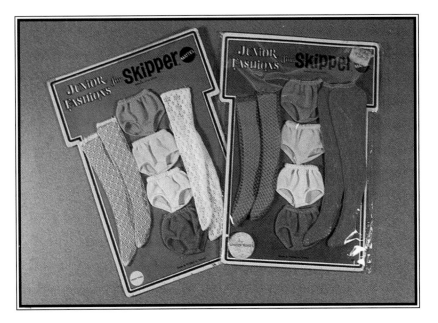

Undertones

Pretty essentials were four pairs of panties in blue, pink, yellow, and white. The two pairs of hose varied as shown. $75.00

Nighty Night

Ready for a slumber party, Skipper doll looked adorable in blue with white polka dots! Her shorty pajamas had lace trim and she wore them with yellow scuffs. Her other accessories were a princess phone and paper "face" mirror with metallic paper mirror. $75.00

Summer Slacks

This one-piece jumpsuit looked like two pieces and came in various fabric combos. Sunglasses and a vinyl belt completed the look. $75.00

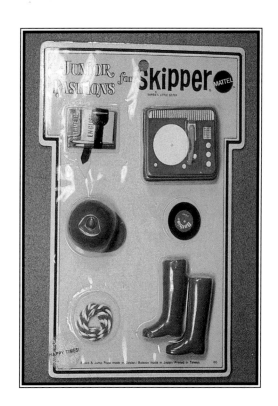

Happy Times!

Ready for fun, pak pieces included a pink and blue record player and Barbie doll record; blue molded vinyl cap and boots; a jump rope; and a stack of books with black vinyl book strap. $75.00

Sears Exclusive
Young Ideas
(1970 – 1973)

This cute set included a faux fur coat with vinyl trim, a three-piece suit with jacket, mini skirt with vinyl waistband and sleeveless knit shell, shorts and ruffled top, pantyhose, knit knee socks, two pairs of shoes, party invitation, golden wrapped gift, and jump rope. $150.00

Sears Exclusive
Living Skipper Doll
Very Best Velvet Set (1970 – 1971)
#1586

A pretty Living Skipper doll came boxed with an orange velvet dress and coat set. The skirt of the dropped waist dress was yellow as was the lining of the coat. The skirt of the dress had a nylon overskirt with orange edging and a blue ribbon waistband. Yellow flats and pantyhose completed the set. $1,500.00

Pretty Pairs

These wonderful characters made great friends for Tutti doll.

Lori 'n Rori Dolls (1970)
#1133 (center)

The pretty blonde was dressed in a pink/white/blue floral and striped feminine dress, white socks and shoes. She had a brown fuzzy teddy bear to love! Outfit and toy only. $50.00

Nan 'n Fran Dolls (1970)
#1134 (left)

The cute floral flannel nightie had a matching night cap, slippers, and a pajama-clad doll's doll! $50.00

Angie 'n Tangie Dolls (1970)
#1135 (right)

Another dressy outfit featured orange and pink with lace, fishnet pantyhose, and shoes with bows. The rag doll picked up the color scheme in her clothing. $50.00

Chapter IV— 1971

Music and Fashion

Music and motion were the key words to describe Barbie doll's world in 1971. The exciting Live Action dolls danced to their own records on their stands or stages in outrageous fringed costumes! Even a clothing line, Fashion 'n Sounds, carried through this theme with records packaged with the costumes. And, Barbie doll's wonderfully articulated horse Dancer pranced on her own stand! Even Barbie doll's Sun 'n Fun Buggy was motorized and had rocking seats! Barbie doll had 32 new Ensemble Paks, three Fashion 'n Motion outfits, and Sears exclusive gift sets. Also, 12 Ensemble Paks from 1970 were repeated. These were Tennis Team #1781, Shape-Ups #1782, Ruffles 'n Swirls #1783, Harem-m-m's #1784, Bright 'n Brocade #1786, Prima Ballerina #1787, Scuba-do's #1788, Fiery Felt #1789, The Lace Caper #1791, Mood Matchers #1792, Skate Mates #1793, and Check The Suit #1794. The six Paks were repeated and there was a new J.C. Penney exclusive accessory pak.

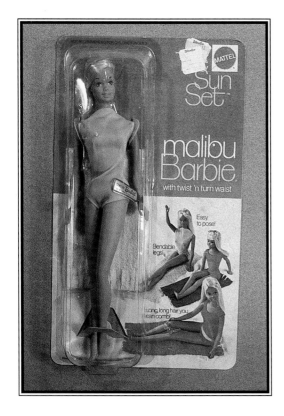

Malibu Barbie Doll (1971 – 1973)
#1067 Original Outfit

A simple blue tricot suit and yellow beach towel sent Barbie doll to Malibu! $25.00

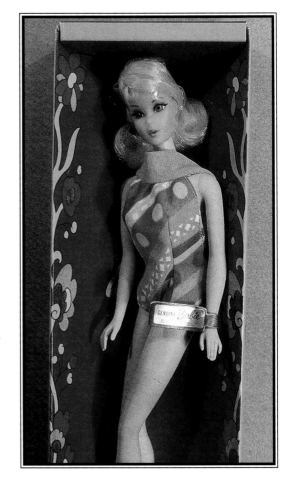

Twist 'n Turn Barbie Doll (1971)
#1160 Original Outfit

The new suit featured diagonal bands of colorful geometrics. The fabric was tricot. $50.00

Talking Barbie Doll
Original Outfit
(1971 – 1973)
#1115

Her swimsuit was a glam-
orous white, leather-look
vinyl two-piece style with
long golden cover-up
with button closure at the
elasticized waist. $45.00

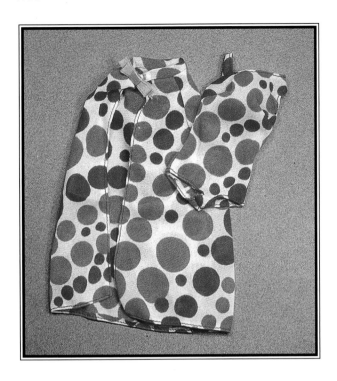

Living Barbie Doll
Original Outfit (1971 – 1972)
#1116

The new outfit featured big dots on a white tricot background. The one shoulder swimsuit had a wraparound skirt for a cover-up. $65.00

Department Store Special
Hair Happenin's Barbie Doll
Original Outfit (1971)
#1174

The lovely doll had three hairpieces and hair accessories and she wore a one-piece tricot dress with black velveteen belt with golden bead button closure. (See color variations on the dress. White with fuchsia was the common version.) Black cut-out shoes and white panties completed the look. $95.00

Barbie Doll With
Growin' Pretty Hair
Original Outfit (1971)
#1144

The lovely doll came with hairpieces and accessories and wore a pink satin dress with attached golden belt. She wore pink chunky shoes. $55.00

These dolls were identical, except one came with a motorized stage and the other came with a Touch 'n Go stand. The outfit was one of the best salutes to the hippie look!

Live Action On Stage
Barbie Doll (1971 – 1972)
#1152;
Live Action Barbie Doll
Original Outfits (1971 – 1973)
#1155 (left)

The tie dye jumpsuit had suedecloth trim and fringe. A suedecloth headband, bracelets with fringe and tan Skipper doll flats completed the set. $45.00

Live Action On Stage P.J. Doll (1971 – 1972)
#1153;
Live Action P.J. Doll
Original Outfits (1971 – 1973)
#1156 (center)

The identical doll wore a red knit mini dress with attached hose and gold fabric (knit or lamé) boots. The second piece of the outfit was a purple suedecloth fringed vest with golden bead button closure. $45.00

Live Action Christie Doll
Original Outfit (1971 – 1973)
#1175 (right)

The purple print tricot two-piece pantsuit was trimmed in purple suedecloth. A purple scarf in Christie doll's hair and chunky shoes completed her ensemble. $55.00

Barbie Doll Ensemble Paks for 1971

Fringe Benefits (1971 – 1972)
#3401

The brightest orange suedecloth added interest to this simple, raspberry knit sheath. The neckline, belt, and fringed boots were fashioned from the contrasting suedecloth. $125.00

Two-Way Tiger (1971 – 1972)
#3402

For this fashion, wild animal print was converted to psychedelic colors of chartreuse and orange! The outfit could be worn as a pantsuit with the wide bell bottom pants and the empire sleeveless top with orange ribbon bow and solid color hem border. Or the top made a great mini dress all by itself. Chartreuse chunky shoes completed the set. $150.00

Baby Doll Pinks (1971 – 1972)
#3403

Barbie doll lit up the night in this bright pink gown of sheer nylon lined with tricot. The gathered bodice ended at an empire waist trimmed with a contrasting red-orange bow of satin ribbon. The straps were ribbon also. The skirt had a self ruffle at the hem. Big, fluffy pink scuffs with nylon bows completed the set. $125.00

Glowin' Out (1971 – 1972)
#3404

This Barbie doll evening dress was short and simple, but nice. The pink, sleeveless satin bodice met a pink and gold brocade skirt. Two pink satin bows adorned the sides of the waist. The outfit was completed with pink chunky shoes. $150.00

Midi Mood (1971 – 1972)
#3407

Unusually conservative for Barbie doll, this two-piece set consisted of a neat, long sleeved blouse with collar, cuffs, and golden bead button accented front. The floral skirt featured a horizontal pleat at the hem and yellow accent stitching. Yellow chunky shoes completed the set. $150.00

Evening In (1971 – 1972)
#3406

1971's version of Dinner At Eight! These lovely, jersey two-piece hostess pajamas featured bright, floral wide leg pants. The hostess dress featured a fitted bodice with set-in waist accented by a large goldtone buckle. The gathered skirt opened to the waist to show off the great pants. Rose cut-out shoes and goldtone triangle earrings completed the ensemble. $150.00

Super Scarf (1971 – 1972)
#3408

Red tricot formed the long sleeved top and the dramatic fringed scarf. The wooly textured skirt had two goldtone bead buttons and chain accent. Red mid-calf boots completed the simple but effective look. $150.00

Red For Rain (1971 – 1972)
#3409

1971's answer to the 1963 raincoat? This updated style featured a collar, belt, and standaway yoke. The belt had a goldtone rectangular buckle. A cute, three corner scarf and white mid-calf rain boots completed the ensemble that would brighten any day! $150.00

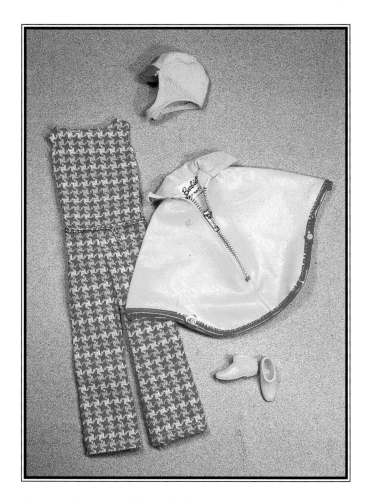

Poncho Put-On (1971 – 1972)
#3411

Barbie doll's great mod outfit featured a yellow/white/orange knit jumpsuit covered by a bright yellow, vinyl zip front poncho with orange trim with two tabs with yellow buttons. A matching yellow knit hat had an orange bill. Yellow go-go boots completed the striking impression. $200.00

Fun Flakes (1971 – 1972)
#3412

Snowflakes, Barbie doll style! They were cerise, of course, and they lined up across the white, wide leg pants as well as accenting the bodice and sleeves of the matching jacket. The jacket also had goldtone bead buttons accenting the front and a cerise tricot stand-up collar that matched the sleeveless shell underneath. Cerise chunky shoes were included. $175.00

Golfing Greats (1971 – 1972)
#3413

What a marvelous set! Barbie doll looked absolutely fabulous on the links in her bright yellow, tricot long sleeved
body blouse. Her wrap golf skirt with vinyl tab and two
golden bead buttons at the waist was fashioned
from a colorful plaid as was her cap with
turquoise vinyl bill and her plastic laminated golf
bag. Her accessories were turquoise knit knee
socks and tennis shoes. Two golf balls and two different golf clubs were included. $225.00

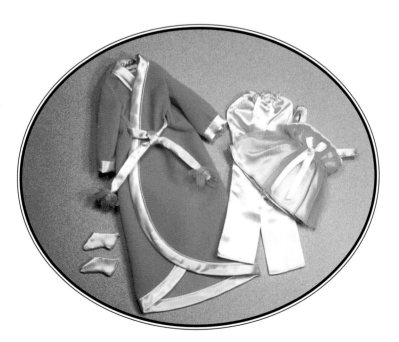

Satin Slumber (1971 – 1972)
#3414

Beautiful, pale blue satin pajamas featured a top
accented with sheer nylon over satin. The matching pants were satin and her robe was a deeper
blue brushed nylon, bound and belted with the
satin. Cute satin slippers were closed toe and heel
construction—not the usual slip-ons or big furry
slippers! Very pretty set. $200.00

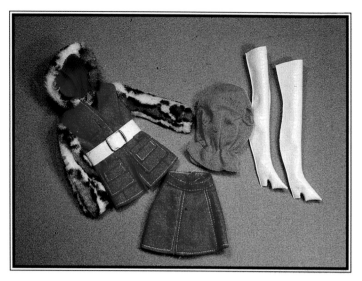

Wild 'n Wintery (1971 – 1972)
#3416

A definite winner from 1971. This wonderful winter suit was fashioned from hot pink felt and was trimmed with nice quality faux leopard on the hood and sleeves. A wide white textured vinyl belt nipped Barbie doll's waist. A knit sleeveless shell provided indoor comfort. Wild, white textured vinyl fashioned the hip boots and matched the belt. $250.00

Bridal Brocade (1971 – 1972)
#3417

One of Barbie doll's loveliest wedding gowns was perfect for a winter wedding! The beautiful brocade fabric formed the gored A-line dress with empire waist, long sleeves and roll collar. Faux fur and gold/white braid accented the cuffs and hem. Barbie doll's headpiece featured a cap of brocade trimmed in front with braid and a double layer of tulle for the veil. She carried a bouquet of white flowers with green net and white satin ribbon streamers. White short gloves and chunky shoes completed the lovely ensemble. $300.00

Magnificent Midi (1971 – 1972) #3418

Another great ensemble that has to be one of the favorites of 1971! The completely coordinated look started with a black, sleeveless high-necked ribbed bodice with a red velvet-look skirt with with black soutache braid and a wide black patent-look attached belt with a circular goldtone buckle. The matching coat featured three black vinyl fasteners at six goldtone buttons. The braid also accented the collar and the cuffs. Black faux fur trimmed the hem, the red hat, and the black patent-look boots. $300.00

Silver Serenade (1971 – 1972) #3419

A long, glittery gown and microphone poised for Barbie doll's solo could describe "Solo In the Spotlight" or in this case "Silver Serenade!" Barbie doll looked magnificient in a silver and turquoise metallic striped-weave fabric. The dress featured a color block technique, slit skirt, silvery braid straps, and flower at the bodice. The wonderful accessories were turquoise nylon pantyhose, cut-out shoes, silvery elbow gloves, and dramatically long turquoise faux fur stole. For her serenade, she had a microphone which was very similar to the one in "Solo In the Spotlight" except it was not marked Japan. $300.00

Bubbles 'n Boots (1971 – 1972)
#3421

One of the prettiest daytime dresses from 1971 featured a colorful print dress with ruffle at the neck and hem of the push-up sleeves. Purple suedecloth fashioned the tall boots and the belt with golden accents that fastened with a single golden bead button. $200.00

The Color Kick (1971 – 1972)
#3422

Horizontal stripes abounded on a technicolor test pattern in Barbie doll's jersey turtleneck top and pantyhose! A bright yellow faux fur skirt wrapped to the side and had three large red accent buttons. $200.00

Night Lighter (1971 – 1972)
#3423

Purple, chartreuse, and red tricot fashioned this jumpsuit with long sleeves and banded neck and pants legs. A purple suedecloth belt with circular goldtone buckle and red go-go boots completed the set. $175.00

Turtle 'n Tights (1971 – 1972)
#3426

Great bright colors worked well together for this swingy salute to fringe! The electric blue turtleneck met matching pantyhose. The bright orange suede-cloth was fringed to mid thigh and had a matching belt. Blue chunky shoes completed the eye-catching ensemble. $175.00

In Blooms (1971 – 1972)
#3424

Barbie doll's bright tricot paisley caftan featured a solid front panel edged in pink for accent. It was quite a different style for Barbie doll! Blue wedge shoes completed the look. $125.00

The Dream Team (1971 – 1972)
#3427

This delicate gown and robe featured a gown of white sheer nylon lined in tricot with a lacy yoke and ruffle and accented with blue satin ribbon. The matching robe was fashioned of lace with a lace ruffle at the neck sleeves. It tied at the waist with a blue satin ribbon. White felt scuffs featured blue ribbon under lace on the strap. $175.00

The Zig Zag Bag (1971 – 1972)
#3428

The creative use of pattern scale in fabric was the highlight of this seldom seen outfit. The red and white zig zag knit formed the bell bottom slacks. A larger, more colorful zig zag pattern formed the blouse. This was topped by a soft red knit pullover. Red chunky shoes completed the ensemble. $175.00

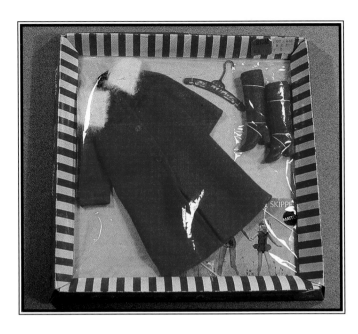

Cold Snap (1971 – 1972)
#3429

1971's "It's Cold Outside"? This red brushed tricot coat had three large red buttons and a white fake fur collar. Red knee high "laced" boots completed the look. $150.00

In Stitches (1971 – 1972)
#3432

A bright print added interest to the heavy, woven cloth. A yellow tricot blouse with long sleeves and tie at the neck contrasted the pants and long vest. Yellow go-go boots and shoulder bag completed the set. $200.00

Victorian Velvet (1971 – 1972)
#3431

An all-time favorite, this opulent dress in rich purple velvet and antique white lace had creamy white sleeves in leg-of-mutton style. Small antique white braid accented the neckline and empire waist and two rows of braid accented the long skirt. Three creamy "pearl" buttons detailed the bodice. Purple cut-out shoes completed the wonderful ensemble. $225.00

All About Plaid (1971 – 1972)
#3433

Bright orange and lime plaid polyester formed the tricolor fringed shawl and V-shaped fringed skirt. The bodice was fashioned of lime knit and featured long sleeves. A wide, orange soft vinyl belt with large circular goldtone buckle accented the dropped waist. Green chunky shoes and a plaid bag with vinyl trim and a golden bead button closure completed the set. $200.00

Fun Fur (1971 – 1972)
#3434

A great coat look was fashioned out of a truly fun fur in shades of beige. The collar and belt were made of warm brown suedecloth. The wide belt had an unusual goldtone buckle. The lace hat looked crocheted with pom pon on the side. Warm brown "laced" knee boots completed the cold weather ensemble! $200.00

Gaucho Gear (1971 – 1972)
#3436

This fabulous set had many great pieces that worked well together. The floral body suit was topped by orange vinyl gauchos trimmed in brown suedecloth. This suedecloth formed the waist length fringed vest, shoulder bag, and boots. A paisley full skirt was also included. An orange felt hat trimmed in golden braid had a green slide on the chin strap. $225.00

Dancing Lights (1971 – 1972)
#3437

Barbie doll's glorious gown was fashioned from a bright print organdy that formed the bodice and the tiered skirt. The dress, except for the sleeves, was lined in fuchsia nylon. Cerise lamé accented the waistline of the bodice and a cerise lamé stole lined in the fuchsia nylon created a nice accessory, as did her black butterfly choker with two yellow beads! Cerise closed toe pumps completed the set. $300.00

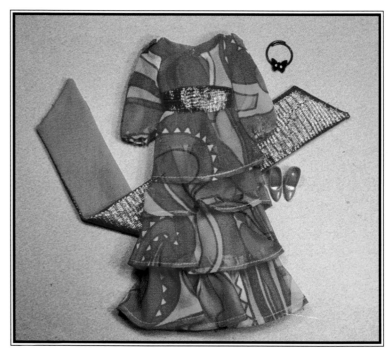

Peasant Dressy (1971 – 1972)
#3438

The best of the peasant look ensembles! The fabulous brushed tricot paisley created the long sleeved and full skirted dress with ruffle trim. Above the purple velvet waistband, the bodice laced with yellow cord, and underneath it all, Barbie doll wore a white full slip with eyelet ruffle at hem, eyelet camisole, yellow cord straps, and tiny bow trim. Brown "laced" knee high boots completed the set. $275.00

Wild Things (1971 – 1972)
#3439

Barbie doll looked great in this bright lime, long sleeved jumpsuit. A royal blue textured vinyl belt fastened with a single golden bead button and accented her tiny waist. A midi length white faux fur vest was trimmed with three rows of floral braid. It was lined in lime green silk. Royal blue go-go boots completed the set. $200.00

Fashion 'n Sounds Outfits for Barbie, P.J. and Christie Dolls!

The latest fashion looks were combined with a real 45 rpm record for these unique ensembles.

Country Music (1971 – 1972)
#1055

This extravagantly ruffled country fashion looked ready for the Grand Old Opry! The blouse featured leg-of-mutton sleeves with ruffled cuffs. A big ruffle stood up for the collar and cascaded down the fitted bodice. A wider ruffle formed the peplum of the blouse. Tiny white rickrack and goldtone bead buttons also trimmed the blouse. The full skirt featured a coordinating white background fabric, eyelet lace and more rickrack. White knee high boots with red painted "laces", a white crocheted-look lace three corner shawl with fringe, red sunglasses and a real 45 rpm with two songs completed the set. $225.00

Groovin' Gauchos (1971 – 1972)
#1057

Wild graphic print on brushed tricot formed the vest and gauchos. The blouse was fashioned from bright fuchsia tricot. A fuchsia suedecloth dog collar choker, fringed shoulder bag, boots and a real two-sided 45 rpm record completed the mod outfit. $225.00

Festival Fashion (1971 – 1972)
#1056

This peasant look had a sheer nylon body blouse lined in tricot and trimmed in lace. The full floral skirt was held with a brown suedecloth laced wide belt and was topped with a pink jersey vest with three large gold-tone buttons. A matching head scarf (really a hat made to look like a tied scarf), dark brown knee high boots, and a real two-sided 45 rpm record completed the gypsy set. $225.00

Barbie Doll's Fashion Paks for 1971

Soft 'n Snug (1971)

The furry skirt featured a satin ribbon waistband and matching bonnet that tied under the chin. Chunky shoes completed the set. $75.00

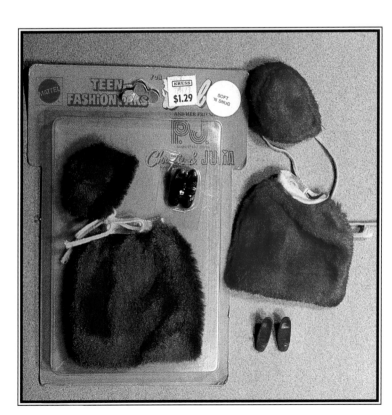

Walking Pretty (1971)

The footwear pak contained tall cerise boots; pink bow shoes; green and white square toe shoes; and red, black, navy, fuchsia, and yellow chunky shoes. $75.00

Cool 'n Casual (1971)

This pak had a halter and slacks made from the same pattern as last year's pak, Cool Casuals. Chunky shoes completed the look. $75.00

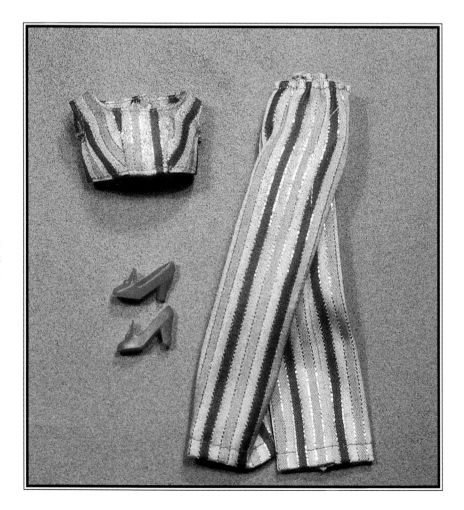

Fashion Firsts (1971)

Pretty lingerie for Barbie doll. Shown are variations of the pak that contained a lace-trimmed petticoat; two pairs of panties; and a fuzzy scale. $75.00

Plush 'n Warm (1971)

Hot pink fleece formed the hooded playsuit that looked great under pants or over a swimsuit! $55.00

The Sew In (1971)

All the notions the Barbie doll seamstress needed! The pak contained two zippers; "pearl" buttons; yellow, orange, blue, and fuchsia flat buttons; red and blue shank buttons; gold and silvertone bead buttons; green and gold marbelized buttons; pink flowers with yellow centers; and two gold-tone and two silvertone belt buckles. $75.00

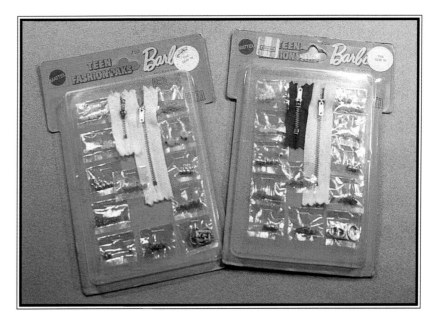

J.C. Penney Exclusive
Made For Malibus
Accessory Pak (1971)
#1497

Contents of this fun accessory pak were
three scarves in blue, green, and yellow; a
paper beach umbrella with wooden stake
and paper ring to hold it closed; colorful
skim board, brown plastic T.V.; red Barbie
doll case; orange vinyl purse with daisy; blue
and hot pink record player; two records;
blue and yellow ball; sailboat; orange
snorkel; face mask and swim fins; pink, red,
and turquoise sunglasses; hamburger on a
white plate; turquoise comb, brush, and mirror; black eyelash brush; blonde hairpiece
with red-orange bow and brass barrette.
$150.00

Sears Exclusive
Talking Barbie Doll
Perfectly Plaid Gift Set
(1971 – 1972)
#1193

Talking Barbie doll's pantsuit was the epitome of the '70s in a huge scale plaid fabric! The one-piece jumpsuit had a red tricot top, plaid pants and attached white vinyl waistband. The plaid coat had a white faux fur collar and matching hat. A white vinyl clutch and red flat shoes completed the set. $1,200.00

Sears Exclusive
Live Action P.J. Doll
Fashion 'n Motion Gift Set (1971 – 1972)
#1508

The cute dancer was dressed in her regular outfit and had another dance scene ensemble. A pretty bright print formed the cropped top with orange suedecloth fringe on the elongated sleeves. The top worked with the matching skirt and pants. Both the pants and the skirt had suedecloth waistbands. Suedecloth boots completed the look. P.J. doll's record and touch 'n go stand were also included. $1,500.00

Ken Doll Ensemble Paks for 1971

Ken doll had six new Ensemble Paks for 1971 featuring a tux, a new ski set, updated business suit, and three casual styles. His Casual All-Stars shown in 1970 was still available exclusively from Sears.

Live Action On Stage
Ken Doll (1971 – 1972)
#1172
Live Action
Ken Doll (1971 – 1973)
#1159

The identical dolls wore mod print tricot shirts, satin pants and suedecloth fringed vests. Brown shoes completed the look. $45.00

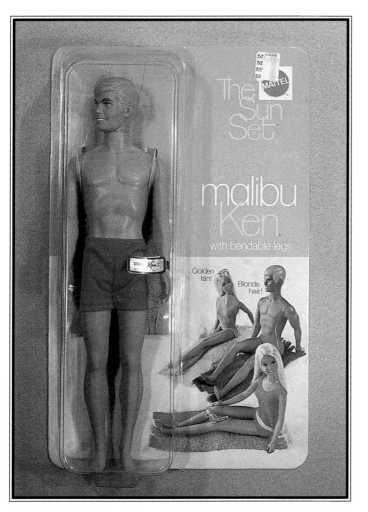

Malibu Ken Doll (1971 – 1974)
#1088

The doll wore red tricot trunks and had a blue beach towel. $25.00

The Skiing Scene (1971 – 1972)
1438

Ken doll looked wonderful in his colorful striped knit sweater and knit cap with red pom pon. He also wore navy slacks, navy ski boots, and red mittens. He had yellow skis and wooden ski poles. $225.00

The Suede Scene (1971 – 1972)
#1439

Ken doll's slacks and vest were fashioned from a warm brown suedecloth that felt almost like rubber! The long sleeved satin shirt featured a medallion print on burgundy. The vest featured a self belt with goldtone buckle and three buttons at the front closure. Gold socks and brown shoes completed the set. $225.00

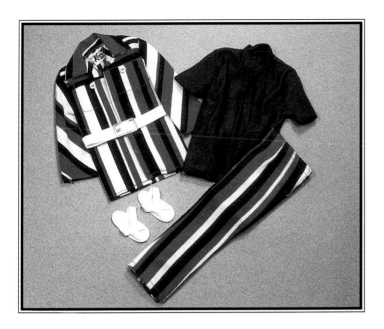

The Casual Scene (1971 – 1972)
#1472

Ready for the 4th of July, Ken doll wore this wild red, white, and blue suit with a white vinyl belt. White buttons accented the breast pockets. Under the smooth textured jacket, he wore matching stripe piqué slacks and a navy tricot shirt. The outfit was completed with white vinyl sandals. $225.00

The Sea Scene (1971 – 1972)
#1449

This cold weather outfit for Ken doll featured a white knit turtleneck with red and blue patterned knit slacks. A warm blue felt pea coat with four white buttons topped it off. Blue tricot socks and white shoes completed this set. $225.00

The V.I.P. Scene (1971 – 1972)
#1473

Ken doll's business suit was updated in both style and fabric. The suit featured double-breasted styling and was made of a red and black plaid. He wore a red-orange shirt and a black and white herringbone tie with the suit. Black shoes and tricot socks completed the set that was ready for business! $225.00

The Night Scene (1971 – 1972)
#1496

What a doll! Ken doll wore his burgundy tux in style! The satin cummerbund and lapels matched the suit perfectly. He sported a white boutonniere on his lapel. The ruffles on his shirt were stitched in burgundy. He completed
the look with an attached black satin bow tie, black shoes and burgundy tricot socks. $225.00

Ken Doll's Fashion Paks for 1971

Sun Fun (1971)

Ken doll's open front summer shirt came in many fabrics. Shown are some examples. A black plastic camera with gray painted trim and green sunglasses completed the set. $75.00

Slacks Are Back (1971)

Ken doll's slacks came with three pairs of tricot socks. $65.00

Golf Gear (1971)

This golf gear was the same as the bag, two clubs and two balls found in Barbie doll's Golfing Greats #3413. $75.00

Shoe ins (1971)

The set included brown cowboy boots; yellow swim fins; white vinyl sandals; and dress shoes in black, white, and brown. $65.00

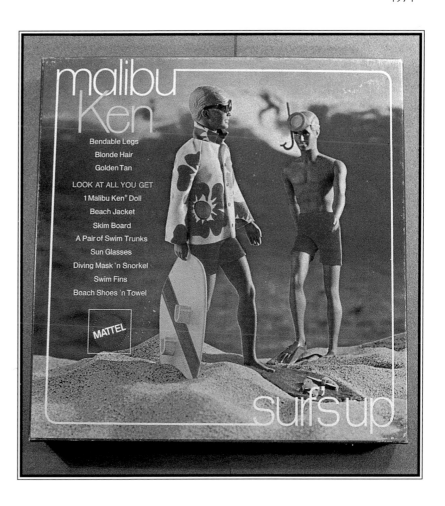

Sears Exclusive
Malibu Ken Doll
Surf's Up Gift Set (1971 – 1972)
#1248

Malibu Ken doll had his red-orange swim trunks and blue towel plus bright floral shirt, matching skim board, blue swim fins, snorkel, face mask, soft yellow sandals, and blue sunglasses. $1,500.00

Skipper Doll's Ensemble Paks for 1971

There were lots of outfits on the market for Skipper doll in 1971. All of her 1970 outfits were still available with the exception of Lots Of Lace #1730, Budding Beauty #1731, Daisy Crazy #1732, and Rik Rak Rah #1733. This included the Paks and the Sears exclusives. Twelve new outfits were introduced in 1971 for Skipper doll and Fluff doll was featured in her own Sears exclusive gift set.

Malibu Skipper Doll (1971 – 1975)
#1069

The cute suntanned doll wore a two-piece orange swimsuit and had a dark blue beach towel. $25.00

Living Skipper Doll (1971 – 1972)
#1117

The beautiful doll had a new yellow lacy swimsuit top over matching panties. She also had a skateboard. $50.00

Living Fluff Doll (1971 – 1972)
#1143

Skipper doll's adorable friend wore a striped knit suit with vinyl overskirt and a skateboard for showing off her poseability! $45.00

Sweet Orange (1971 – 1972)
#3465

Pretty party dress in orange velvet with lace detailing on the sleeves, collar, hem, down the bodice, and forming the belt. White flats completed the set. $150.00

Tennis Time (1971 – 1972)
#3466

Fresh white fabric formed Skipper doll's tennis dress with attached shorts trimmed in pink. The set looked great on the Living dolls. White tennis shoes, socks, racquet, and ball completed the set. $125.00

Teeter Timers (1971 – 1972)
#3467

Great for fun and games, this two-piece set featured a yellow sleeveless blouse with pink floral pockets and neck band. The floral was used for the slacks as well. Yellow flats were included. The teeter totter was formed from yellow plastic with pink tension straps. $175.00

Little Miss Midi (1971 – 1972)
#3468

The pretty, bright green long sleeved blouse with pink buttons was topped by a yellow ground floral print skirt. Turquoise boots completed Skipper doll's grown-up look. $150.00

Ice-Skatin' (1971 – 1972)
#3470

White faux fur formed the bonnet and trimmed the red brushed skating dress. Three white shank buttons trimmed the neckline. Red tricot tights and white skates completed the look. $150.00

Ballerina (1971 – 1972)
#3471

A lovely medley of rose, pale pink, and blue tulle formed the tutu of Skipper doll's ballet costume. The rose tulle created her flutter sleeves on the blue satin costume. A blue satin toe shoe bag, palest pink ballet slippers, and pale pink pantyhose completed the ensemble. $150.00

Double Dashers (1971 – 1972)
#3472

Navy and red-orange knit fabric created the coat for Skipper doll's ensemble. The trim was red-orange vinyl with golden bead buttons. Her dress was fashioned from solid red-orange woven fabric with a navy vinyl placket accented with golden bead buttons. Red-orange flats completed the set. $175.00

Lullaby Lime (1971 – 1972)
#3473

A nice color combination was created with the use of a soft, lime green sheer nylon lined in tricot with hot pink ribbon trim on the bodice. Felt slippers with green nylon ruffles on top completed the set. $150.00

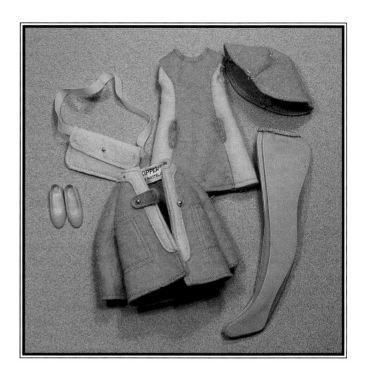

Goin' Sleddin' (1971 – 1972)
#3475

Skipper doll hit the icy hills in great style with a yel-low fun fur hooded jacket with hot pink braid trim and zippered front. Hot pink textured slacks and pink snow boots completed her look. A coordinating pink and yellow plastic sled was also included. $175.00

All Over Felt (1971 – 1972)
#3476

Felt can be boxy and drab but this set with the com-bination of powder blue and bright yellow looked great on Skipper doll. Her dress was topped by a jacket with yellow trim and a tab closure with two goldtone bead buttons. Her matching hat, a yellow felt shoulder bag, and powder blue flats and panty-hose completed the set. (Keep it safe from moths!) $175.00

Dressed In Velvet (1971 – 1972)
#3477

A lovely outfit ready for a chilly day featured a dress with white bodice and pink "velvet" skirt with bright green ribbon and white braid trim at the dropped waist and braid at the neckline. The pink "velvet" coat had a huge collar with white faux fur trim. The hat matched and was fashioned of both the "velvet" and the faux fur. White flats and pale pink stockings completed the ensemble ready for a birthday party! $175.00

Long 'n Short Of It (1971 – 1972)
#3478

A nice '70s color combination was used in the tricot pieces. This fabric fashioned the simple mini dress and extra-long fringed scarf. A red maxi coat with goldtone bead buttons, a white knit tam with red stripes and red pom pon, and red boots completed the set. Shown are variations of the tricot; either red, white, and cerise or red, white, and blue in two different prints. $175.00

Skipper Doll's Fashion Paks from 1971

Skimmer 'n Scarf (1971)

The cute summer dress was fashioned in a light-weight cotton. The empire waist was defined by ribbon. A matching three corner scarf completed the set. Shown are two patterns of fabric. $65.00

Sporty Shorty (1971)

A cute and cool look featured a full mini skirt and crop top with ruffle in a summer-weight fabric. Contrasting flats were included. $65.00

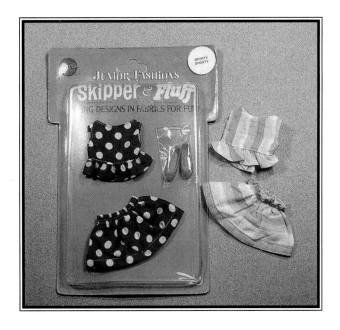

Check The Suit (1971)

Cute, high-waisted flared leg pants had button detailing on each side of the front. Flats were included. $65.00

The Slumber Party (1971)

The fleecy robe had a cord tie belt and lace trim. $65.00

Action Fashions (1971)

The fun pak contained roller skates; ice skates; ballet slippers; rain boots; tennis shoes; flats; jump rope and ball. $65.00

Some Shoes (1971)

The pak contained go-go boots in red, green, and fuchsia; flats in white, orange, yellow, and royal; and red rain boots. $65.00

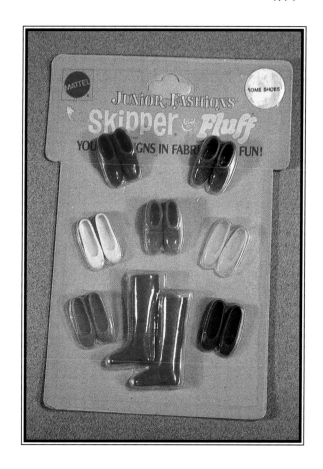

Sears Exclusive
Fluff Doll
Sunshine Special
Gift Set (1971)
#1249

The cute friend of Skipper doll had her own adorable gift set with rickrack-trimmed mix and match pieces. Her white long sleeved blouse teamed with a gold vest and either red slacks or a print full skirt. She also had a dual purpose midriff/scarf, gold opaque tricot pantyhose, and gold flats as well as her original swimsuit and yellow skateboard. $1,500.00

Francie Doll's Looks from 1971

Malibu Francie Doll (1971 – 1975)
#1068

She wore a pink and red tricot suit with yellow belt and had a terry towel. $25.00

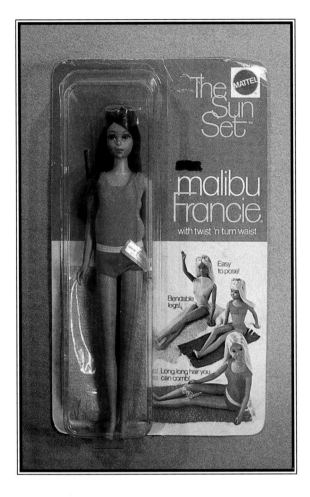

Malibu Francie Doll
From The Foreign Market (1971)
#11068

This beautiful Francie doll wore the same swimsuit as her blonde U.S. counterpart. Outfits only, $25.00

Twist 'n Turn
Francie Doll (1971)
#1170

"No bangs" Francie doll, as she is referred to by collectors, wore an orange, pleated swim dress with white vinyl trim and orange panties. She also had white buckle shoes. $75.00

Francie Doll's Ensemble Paks for 1971

All 16 of the Ensemble Paks introduced for Francie doll in 1970 were still on the market as were the six Paks and Sears Exclusive Pretty Power. In 1971, there were 16 Ensemble Pak fashions and a new Sears Exclusive Gift Set.

Satin Supper (1971 – 1972)
#3443

A pretty hostess ensemble featured a sky blue satin sleeveless jumpsuit topped by a green lace sleeveless vest with satin tie belt. Green square toe pumps completed the ensemble. $150.00

Zig Zag Zoom (1971 – 1972)
#3445

This wonderfully hip outfit featured a yellow ribbed poor boy top with royal vinyl belt with goldtone buckle. The wildest zig zag fabric fashioned the wide leg pants and the cap with royal vinyl bill. Go-go boots and sunglasses or a transistor radio with silvertone antenna and painted trim completed the set. $200.00

Midi Plaid (1971 – 1972)
#3444

This midi dress featured a red tricot, long sleeved bodice with fringed scarf and a big textured plaid skirt. A wide white vinyl belt with goldtone buckle and red square toe pumps completed the set. $150.00

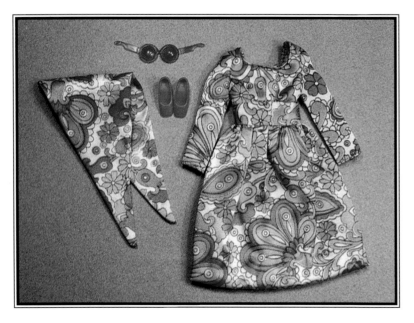

Midi Bouquet (1971 – 1972)
#3446

A floral and paisley medley on satin fashioned a beautiful full skirted, long sleeved dress for the lovely Francie doll. A matching three corner shawl, rose colored sunglasses, and square toe pumps completed the ensemble. $200.00

With It Whites (1971 – 1972, 1974)
#3448

White piqué stitched in red and accented with goldtone bead buttons created three of the pieces of this versatile outfit. The slacks, a long sleeveless tunic top with red vinyl belt, and a red tricot sleeveless shell created lots of looks. Red square toe pumps completed the look. $175.00

Buckaroo Blues (1971 – 1972, 1974)
#3449

Turquoise suedecloth formed this cute western influenced ensemble. The midi skirt was trimmed with white braid and buttons. The same braid detailed the short vest and the boots. The shoulder bag was also made from the suedecloth and featured fringe trim and white button detailing. A red print long sleeved blouse completed the look. $175.00

Dreamy Duo (1971 – 1972, 1974)
#3450

The combination of a mini gown and a maxi robe in sunshine yellow scattered with hot pink floral trim suited Francie doll perfectly. The gown featured a ruffle at the neckline and was lined in tricot. The long robe was fashioned of sheer nylon and was lined with tricot also. It had ruffle trim at the neck and the hem in addition to the braid trim. $175.00

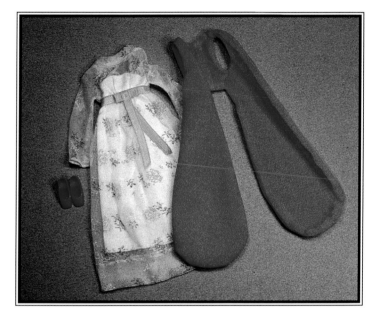

Midi Duet (1971 – 1972, 1974)
#3451

A very pretty and delicate midi ensemble featured a pink and green print sheer white organdy dress with nylon lining and long sleeves with a pink satin ribbon at the empire waist. Pink organdy lined in nylon formed the midi length vest. Pink square toe pumps completed the lovely ensemble. $200.00

Snooze News (1971 – 1972, 1974)
#3453

Hot pink shorty p.j.s featured lavish lace trim on the nylon top lined in tricot. The outfit had matching panties, pink felt scuffs with silvertone bead buttons and a paper face mirror with metallic paper "mirror." $150.00

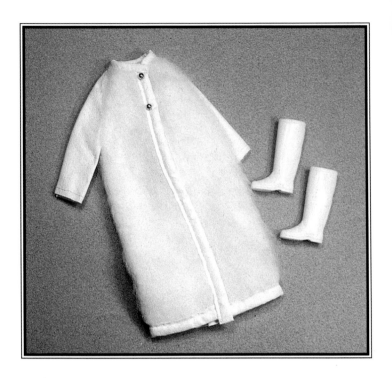

Frosty Fur (1971 – 1972, 1974)
#3455

Snowy white faux fur formed Francie doll's midi coat trimmed in matching textured vinyl and two goldtone bead buttons at the neck. White boots completed the cozy look. $150.00

Summer Number (1971 – 1972, 1974)
#3454

Francie doll looked brighter than the summer sun in this hot pink two-piece swimsuit with yellow, orange, and cerise braid trim. The skirt was fashioned of a bright, bold print and featured a yarn tie at the waist. Pale pink sunglasses completed the ensemble. $175.00

Wild Flowers (1971 – 1972, 1974)
#3456

A pretty printed tricot fashioned this midi dress that looked great on Francie doll. The fitted bodice had a gathered skirt and leg-of-mutton sleeves. Pink square toe pumps completed the set. $150.00

Olde Look (1971 – 1972)
#3458

Oh, what a marvelous ensemble! Francie doll's peasant look featured a pretty floral print on a white ground in the long sleeved maxi dress. Orange crochet-type lace accented the bodice, hem, the matching apron, and the felt basket she carried. An orange weskit with yellow laces cinched her waist. Orange square toe shoes completed the coordinated look. $250.00

Twilight Twinkle (1971 – 1972)
#3459

Francie doll's most elegant ensemble of 1971 featured a turquoise and silver lace over turquoise satin gown. Silvery braid accented the neckline, empire waist, and long sleeves. Turquoise faux fur formed the long, sleeveless maxi vest that was also accented with silvery braid and two silvertone bead buttons. A silvertone clutch bag, flexible vinyl tiara, and blue square toe pumps were the finishing touches. $250.00

1971

Change Offs (1971 – 1972)
#3460

Beautiful dark rose felt edged in a gorgeous floral brocade braid created the ensemble. The coat featured braid down the front, at the waist, and three rows at the hem. The skirt had a front slit accented by the braid that continued around the hem. A pretty, sleeveless satin shell, a tan crocheted-look tam and dark rose "laced" knee-high boots completed the set. $250.00

Peach Plush (1971 – 1972)
#3461

Another favorite from 1971! This versatile outfit featured three pieces fashioned from a colorful, heavy weave stripe and diamond design fabric. The cute jacket, pants, and midi skirt had yellow vinyl trim. The set had a golden yellow, sleeveless knit shell and yellow vinyl "laced" boots. $250.00

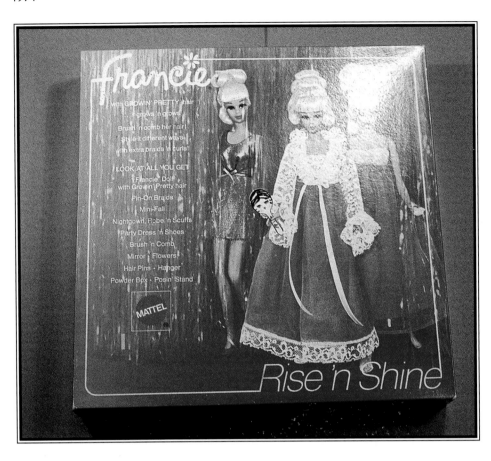

Sears Exclusive
Rise 'n Shine
Francie Doll
Gift Set (1971)
#1194

The pretty Growin' Pretty Hair Francie doll had a lacy, feminine peignoir set. The pink nylon gown and robe were lavishly trimmed with white lace. The robe had satin ribbon bows on the sleeves and it tied at the empire waist. The gown was lined in tricot. Also included were a paper face mirror, comb, brush, Barbie pins, hair flowers, powder box, and white felt scuffs with pink nylon pom pons. The doll wore her usual dress and pumps and had her two hairpieces. $1,500.00

Chapter V – 1972
A Year in Movement

Movement was still an integral component of the dolls introduced in 1972. The wonderful Walk Lively and Busy dolls featured new articulation. And, Pose 'n Play Skipper doll had great fun on her Swing-A-Rounder Gym! The outfits were fabulous and some were available only in 1972 and are the harder to find issues of the 1970s. New friends were introduced: the beautiful Steffie and Miss America dolls and the adorable Tiff doll. The outfit collections were renamed; Fashion Originals were the more accessorized and expensive outfits and Best Buys were simple, but still had flair.

There were lots of repeats from 1971. All of Barbie doll's costumes, with the exception of J.C. Penney Sun Set Accessories, were repeated in 1972. Besides the repeats, she had 34 new outfits. Miss America doll had three of her own and Jamie doll was featured in a new Sears exclusive gift set. Ken doll's six outfits from 1971 were repeated and he had 11 new styles in 1972. All of Francie doll's 1971 costumes were repeated and she had 18 new ones in 1972. Skipper doll's costumes from 1971 were repeated and 10 new ones were added in 1972.

Walk Lively
Barbie Doll
Original Outfit (1972 – 1973)
#1182

The beautiful doll wore a red tricot pantsuit with double belts and a yellow vinyl purse plus red chunky shoes. $45.00

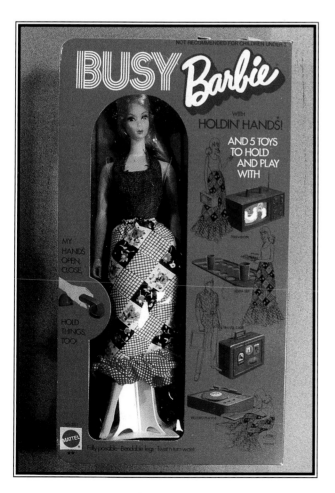

Busy Barbie Doll
Original Outfit (1972 – 1973)
#3311

All of the Busy and Talking Busy dolls had the same busy accessories which were brown plastic T.V., record player, carry case, and a tray and glasses with stick-on decal accents. The outfit Barbie doll wore was a denim top bodysuit with patchwork print maxi skirt. She also had square toe shoes and a tiny brass barrette in her hair. $45.00

Talking Busy Barbie Doll (1972 – 1973)
#1195

Hot pants in blue satin combined with a red tricot top were electrified with a chartreuse belt and knee boots. Brown plastic Busy accessories were included. They were TV, record player, carry case, and tray with glasses. $65.00

Growin' Pretty Hair
Barbie Doll (1972 – 1973)
#1144

The lovely doll had a hairdo and outfit change. The red, white, and blue peasant dress had a laced, blue suede-cloth bodice. Hairpieces and blue square toe shoes were included. $85.00

Forget Me Nots
Barbie Doll (1972)
#3269

The promotional doll was identical to Malibu Barbie doll #1067.
$25.00

Ward's Re-issue
Barbie Doll (1972 – 1973)
#3210

The Montgomery Ward exclusive doll wore a reproduction of
the first black and white swimsuit and white open toe shoes.
$45.00

Walk Lively
Miss America Doll
(1972 – 1973)
#3200
and
Kellogg's Mail-In Offer
Miss America Doll (1972)
#3194 – 9991
Original Outfits

The pretty doll wore a
regal white gown with
nylon overskirt and
gold lamé bodice with
satin ribbon sash. Her
silver mesh (braid)
attached crown,
scepter, red fleece-
like cape with faux fur
trim, and white chunky
shoes completed the
set. $45.00

Walk Lively
Steffie Doll
Original Outfit (1972 – 1973)
#1183 (right)

The gorgeous doll wore a bright one-piece jumpsuit with
nylon scarf at the neck and red chunky shoes. $45.00

Busy Steffie
Original Outfit (1972)
#3312 (above)

Busy Steffie doll wore a long peasant dress in
coordinating calico prints. Square toe shoes
completed the outfit. $45.00

Talking Busy
Steffie Doll
Original Outfit (1972)
#1186 (right)

She wore blue hot pants attached to a pink and white gingham jersey long sleeved blouse with matching stirrup leggings
over white square toe pumps. She had a contrasting black and
white small check belt and hat. Brown plastic TV, record player, carry case, and tray with glasses were included. $65.00

Malibu P.J. Doll
Original Outfit (1972 – 1975)
#1187

A lavender, one-piece suit in tricot was accented with a green towel. $25.00

Barbie Doll's Fashion Originals From 1972

Fun Shine (1972)
#3480

A unique, short evening ensemble featured silver square print lamé fashioned into a full skirt with orange cords accenting the wide, silvertone braid waistband. The long sleeved ruffled front sheer nylon blouse had an attached silver lamé "bra" and orange cord tied at the flowing ruffle collar. Orange pantyhose and chunky shoes completed the set. $250.00

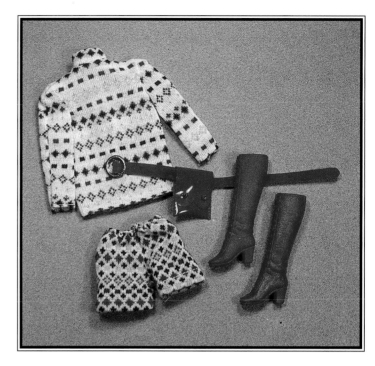

The Short Set (1972)
#3481

Two wonderful coordinating patterns in knit formed the hot pants and the long sleeved tunic in this ensemble. A red vinyl hip belt with goldtone buckle had an attached purse with two goldtone bead buttons. Red vinyl "laced" knee boots completed the set. $200.00

Peasant Pleasant (1972)
#3482

Very down-played peasant inspiration in this orange rick-rack trimmed, tan burlap-look wrap skirt with orange tricot blouse with heavy braid accents. Wedgies with orange vinyl straps and orange leg ties added a funky look! $200.00

Purple Pleasers (1972)
#3483

The purple tricot blouse had accent gathering that created an old-fashioned silhouette. A maxi skirt in a warm print tricot was styled with a ruffle at the hem. Purple chunky shoes completed the set. $175.00

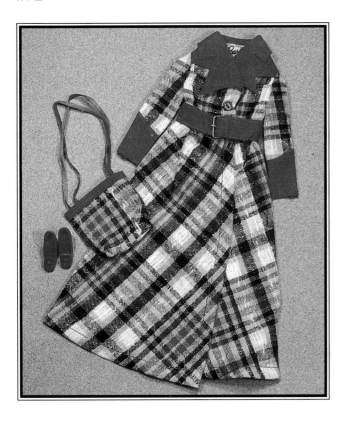

Madras Mod (1972)
#3485

A maxi coat that really said the '70s was this big plaid fabric style that was accented with red velveteen collar, cuffs, and belt. Red chunky shoes and a matching shoulder bag completed the set. $200.00

O-Boy Corduroy (1972)
#3486

This great outfit featured a granny style high neck blouse in dark blue crepe with white ribbon and red single accent "brooch" at the neck. The maxi red corduroy jumper featured crocheted style braid on the bib. White knee boots with red "laces" completed the set. $225.00

Sleepy Set (1972)
#3487

A pink, shorty gown in sheer nylon was lined with tricot and had a floral stripe bodice. The lovely print cotton robe tied with contrasting green satin ribbon. White felt scuffs with pink nylon pom pons completed the ensemble. $200.00

Overall Denim (1972)
#3488

This cute set of overalls actually hooked realistically at the bib! The red tricot tee shirt had contrasting sleeves. A brown, leather-look vinyl backpack and tennis shoes completed the casual set. $200.00

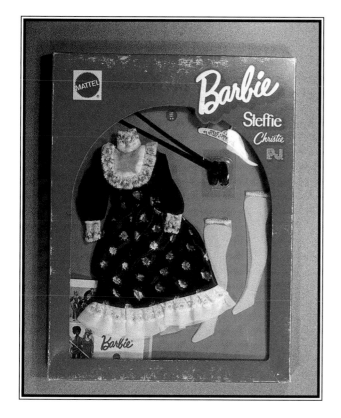

Party Lines (1972)
#3490

A really beautiful dress in black satin with a floral print, sheer black sleeves, sheer white yoke, and lace trim. Black flats with ribbon ties and white hose completed the wonderful fashion. $275.00

Suede 'n Fur (1972)
#3491

Lots of pieces created this ensemble. The taupe suedecloth was used to create the wrap skirt with three goldtone bead buttons and the trim on the midi length faux fur coat. The coat closed with tabs and three goldtone bead buttons. A red tricot cat suit tied color from head to toe! Brown knee boots completed the handsome ensemble. Shown are variations of the coat. $250.00

Flying Colors (1972)
#3492

A hard one to find! The delicate
textured knit, tie front midriff top was
accented with an orange faux fur vest with
hot pink vinyl trim and a single golden bead button. The permanently crinkled skirt featured wild colors in a horizontal design and a hot pink vinyl waistband. A flower on a plastic choker necklace and hot pink chunky shoes
completed this rare ensemble. $300.00

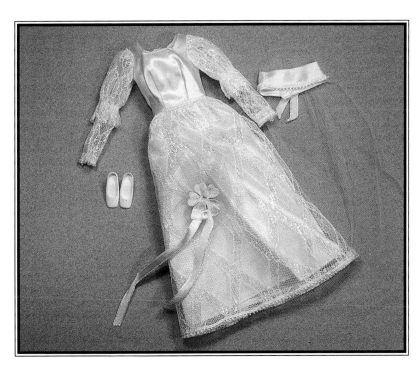

Satin 'n Shine (1972)
#3493

A hard-to-find wedding dress featured
sheer white-on-white, large shiny diagonal
design lace fabric over a satin lining for the
skirt. The satin bodice had the diagonal lace
fabric leg-of-mutton sleeves. A braid-
trimmed satin headpiece with tulle veil, a
bouquet with a single pink flower, green
tulle, and a white satin bow and square toe
pumps completed the ensemble. $300.00

Barbie Doll's Best Buy Fashions for 1972

Furry 'n Fun (1972)
#3336

The red knit maxi coat featured a white faux fur collar,
cuffs, and a red vinyl belt. Gray, knee-high boots completed the set. $75.00

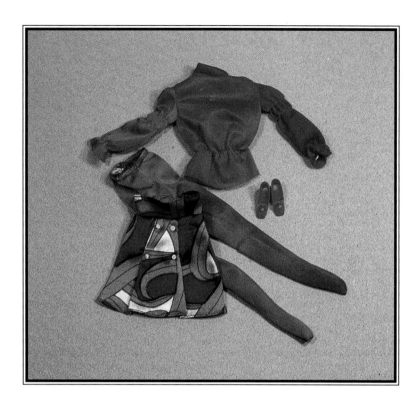

All American Girl (1972)
#3337

The pretty royal blue tricot blouse had sleeve interest with mid-sleeve and waist gathers and ruffled cuffs. The large print satin mini skirt had four white buttons. Blue tricot tights and red chunky shoes completed the ensemble. $75.00

Mainly For Rain (1972)
#3338

Barbie doll looked less dramatic than usual in her red and blue houndstooth flannel coat and hat. The coat featured blue braid trim and buttons. Red knee-high "laced" boots completed the set. Shown are variations in the fabric with one including black as an extra color in the fabric print. This set coordinated with Long 'n Fringy #3341. $75.00

Light 'n Lazy (1972)
#3339

This hard-to-find set included a gown in white, sheer nylon with tricot lining. Lace trimmed the gown, panties, and robe and a thin purple ribbon accented the gown. Booties with lace trim completed the set. $75.00

Long 'n Fringy (1972)
#3341

A yellow tricot long sleeved blouse featured a tie at the high neck and was worn with a larger print flannel maxi skirt with three goldtone bead buttons and fringe at the wrap. Black chunky shoes completed the set. This set coordinated with Mainly For Rain #3338. $75.00

Golden Glitter (1972)
#3340

This ensemble usually looks pretty bad if you find it used! The golden satin did not wear well. The fitted bodice had a sheer yellow stand-up ruffle at the neck and forming the yoke which was accented by goldtone buttons. Gold braid accented the waist. A matching purse and yellow pantyhose and tan square toe pumps completed the set. $75.00

Sweet Dreams (1972)
#3350

These print p.j.s and felt slippers were fit for a slumber party with Skipper doll who just happened to have a matching pair in her Super Snoozers #3371 and Francie doll who had Sleepy Time Gal #3364. $50.00

Good Sports (1972)
#3351

This casual ensemble featured bell bottom jeans, a dark cerise sleeveless tricot top, print three corner scarf, brown vinyl belt, red round sunglasses, and tennis shoes. $75.00

White 'n With It (1972)
#3352

White piqué was unusually dressy when accented with a goldtone front belt, white chunky shoes, and a golden knit bag with chain shoulder strap. $75.00

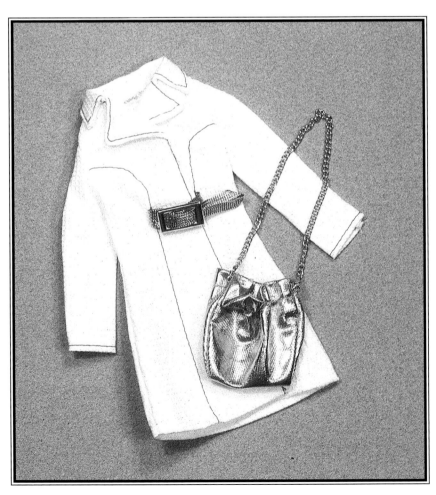

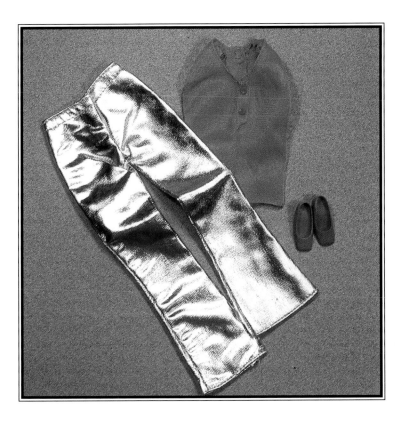

Glowin' Gold (1972)
#3354

A simple sleeveless turquoise shell with two shank button accents was sparked to life when Barbie doll teamed it with golden knit slacks and turquoise square toe shoes. $50.00

Sport Star (1972)
#3353

This cute turquoise denim-look mini skirt had a bib front with white buttons. The contrasting body suit had big puffy sleeves in a star print. Blue chunky shoes completed the set. $100.00

Picture Me Pretty (1972)
#3355

Barbie doll's cute short peasant dress featured a subdued print with full mini skirt, white sleeves, and eyelet lace at the neckline and hem. Lace-trimmed white panties, half slip, and purple chunky shoes completed the set. $75.00

Silver Blues (1972)
#3357

This outfit was made to coordi-
nate with Fancy That Purple
#3362. This evening coat was
fashioned of a pretty goldtone and pastel brocade
with a golden knit bodice.
A sheer purple scarf and
cut out shoes completed
this half of the ensemble!
$125.00

Fancy That Purple (1972)
#3362

This set coordinated with
Silver Blues #3357. The
purple velveteen blouse
topped gold knit hot pants
and/or a long brocade
skirt. Purple pantyhose and
cut out shoes completed
the set. $125.00

Lovely 'n Lavender (1972)
#3358

A pretty sleep set in the palest of pinkish lavender sheer nylon with a tricot lining in the gown.
The bodice featured vertical gathers, an empire
waist, and ruffle at the hem. The dotted nylon
robe had a white faux fur collar and lace trim.
Pink open toe shoes completed the set. A white
pitcher and cup were included. $100.00

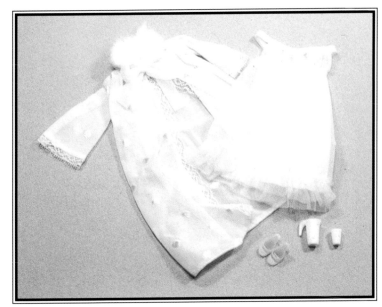

Pants – Perfect Purple (1972)
#3359

This rust colored variegated knit featured a long sleeved
top over bell bottom pants. Adding interest was a faux
leopard fur bag with black patent vinyl trim and black
chunky shoes. $100.00

Pleasantly Peasanty (1972)
#3360

A red floral print formed this maxi length
peasant dress with lace trim at the neckline
and ruffled cuffs. The hem had a wide self
ruffle and Barbie doll's waist was cinched by
a black velveteen belt. A white petticoat
with eyelet lace and black chunky shoes
completed the set. $100.00

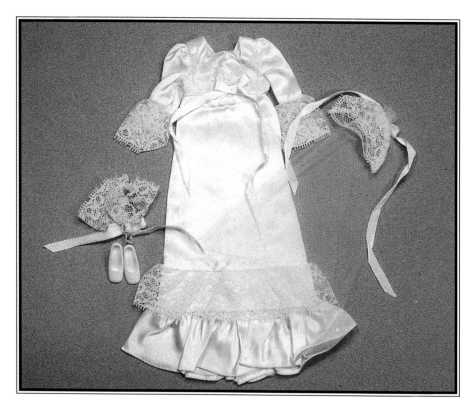

Sweetheart Satin (1972)
#3361

A very hard-to-find wedding dress for Barbie doll was simple, but nice, in white satin with a ruffled hem and wide lace trim above the ruffle and forming cuffs on her sleeves. A bow accented the empire waist. The lace headpiece had a tulle veil and she carried a bouquet of three pink puff flowers, lace, and ribbon. White square toe pumps completed the set. $250.00

Shoe Scene (1972)
#3382

The set contained square toe pumps in royal, yellow, red-orange, and lime; chunky shoes in yellow and black; wedgies in white, red, melon, and pink; "laced" front knee boots in red, white, and navy. $50.00

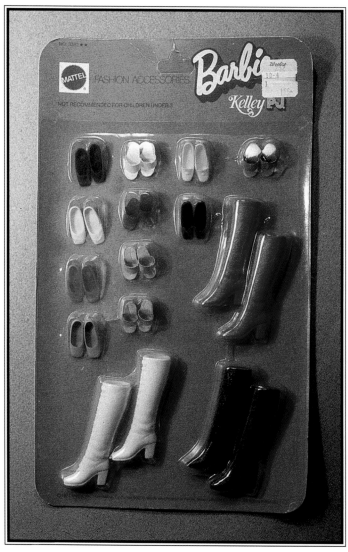

Put-Ons 'N Pets

These three wonderful outfits combined a creative costume with a pet for Barbie doll. They have always been very hard to find.

Poodle Doodles (1972)
#1061

Barbie doll walked her black poodle with blue suede-cloth collar and chain leash with turquoise suedecloth handle. Barbie doll wore a red dress with tricot bodice and floral print skirt, boots, and short jacket with turquoise suedecloth collar and waistband. $350.00

Kitty Kapers (1972)
1062

The best cat Barbie doll ever had! This white Persian had blue bead eyes and pink sewn nose and mouth. Barbie doll's summery outfit was fashioned of three colors of polka dot tricot and trimmed in white rick-rack. The long sleeve top revealed a bit of midriff over either the hot pants or long skirt. White "laced" knee boots and a yellow bowl with "food" for Kitty completed the set. $350.00

Hot Togs (1972)
#1063

What a dog! Barbie doll's elegant Afghan hound was led on a brown suedecloth leash and collar. Barbie doll's outfit was smashing and so indicative of the times. The bold plaid jacket topped red cuffed hot pants! She wore olive pantyhose and thigh-high knit socks, brown "laced" knee-high boots and a brown suedecloth belt with attached purse with red button. An olive knit cap completed the set. $350.00

Miss America Doll's Fashions for 1972

Royal Velvet (1972)
#3215

This wonderful rose velvet gown featured leg-of-mutton sleeves, full skirt, and white faux fur at the neckline. A bright fuchsia, sheer nylon long slip with hem ruffle, white faux fur muff, and rose chunky shoes completed the set. $350.00

Majestic Blue (1972)
#3216

This beautiful turquoise sheer nylon gown was lined with silk and featured a ruffled peplum and skirt ruffle. Her white faux fur jacket was lined in turquoise silk and edged in golden braid. A bouquet of five hot pink fabric roses with leaves, green tulle, and a Miss America ribbon banner tying them together, white long gloves, and turquoise chunky shoes completed the lovely ensemble. $350.00

Regal Red (1972)
#3217

A lovely red-orange satin was used for the dress and cape in this lovely ensemble. Golden knit formed the bodice and yellow real fur accented the cape. A golden belt with square buckle accented the waist. Hard-to-find bright yellow long gloves, a golden clutch, and red square toe shoes completed the set. $350.00

Sears Exclusive Strollin' In Style Jamie Doll Gift Set (1972) #1247

The beautiful Jamie doll wore a color variation of her usual original outfit. In this giftset, the dress was blue, yellow, and red. She had a blue scarf and red boots with the pretty blue knit pantsuit with yellow trim, crocheted belt, and chunky shoes. Her charming white furry poodle had a blue suedecloth collar and a blue and yellow ball. $1,500.00

Ken Doll's Fashions for 1972

All of Ken doll's outfits from 1971 were repeated and he had great new ensembles for 1972!

Walk Lively
Ken Doll
Original Outfit (1972 – 1973)
#1184

Casual good looks combined in a blue knit shirt and big plaid pants with brown shoes. $50.00

Busy Ken Doll
Original Outfit (1972)
#3314

A red, textured knit tank top with brown vinyl belt topped blue jeans and tennis shoes. He also had Busy accessories, brown plastic TV, record player, carry case, and tray with glasses. $45.00

Talking Busy
Ken Doll
Original Outfit (1972)
#1196

A red and blue tiny print shirt topped blue slacks. A belt, shoes, and his Busy accessories, a brown plastic TV, record player, carry case, and tray with glasses, completed the look. $50.00

Ken Doll's Fashion Originals For 1972

Casual Cords (1972)
#1717

Ken doll's great looking outfit featured a print shirt topped by a blue knit belted sweater. He wore gold cord slacks, socks, and brown shoes. $175.00

Brown On Brown (1972)
#1718

This nice looking suit featured a brown jacket over tan slacks with a chartreuse stripe and floral short sleeve shirt and yellow tie. Tan socks and brown shoes completed the hard-to-find set. $200.00

Midnight Blues (1972)
#1719

Ken doll's tux jacket was fashioned of midnight blue silk with black satin lapels and was worn with black, elastic back slacks. The tux was accessorized by a white tricot dress shirt and attached black tie, socks, and shoes. $200.00

Way Out West (1972)
#1720

Ken doll's matching set included a jeans jacket and pants. A red three corner tricot neckerchief and brown cowboy boots completed the look. $175.00

Mod Madras (1972)
#1828

This very '70s leisure suit featured loud plaid slacks, an ochre jacket with buttons on the breast pockets, and burgundy vinyl belt. A burgundy tricot shirt and vinyl sandals completed the outfit. Shown are two examples. $200.00

Ken Doll's Best Buy Fashions for 1972

Ken doll Best Buy Fashions apply only to top left and bottom photos on this page.

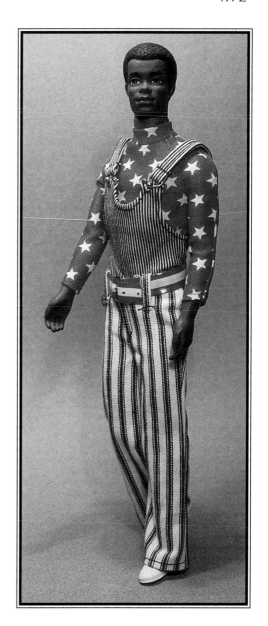

Denims For Fun (1972)
#3376

Big cargo pockets highlighted Ken doll's jeans. A red, white, and blue shirt and white shoes completed the outfit. $75.00

Red, White & Wild (1972)
#1829

This outfit was about as patriotic as you can get! Ken doll wore a star print red tricot shirt with blue and white striped slacks and a thin blue striped sleeveless vest with suspenders. White tennis shoes and a red and white wide vinyl belt were finishing touches. $200.00

Wide Awake Stripes (1972)
#3377

Ken doll rested easily in a blue brushed robe with striped collar that matched his pajama bottoms. The robe also had a tie belt. White vinyl sandals (slippers) completed the set. $75.00

Western Winner (1972)
#3378

A khaki jacket with self belt and pocket tabs topped pants with wide stripes. Cowboy boots completed the set. $75.00

Cool 'n Casual (1972)
#3379

A blue long sleeved shirt paired with small checked pants along with a burgundy tie, burgundy socks, and black shoes. $75.00

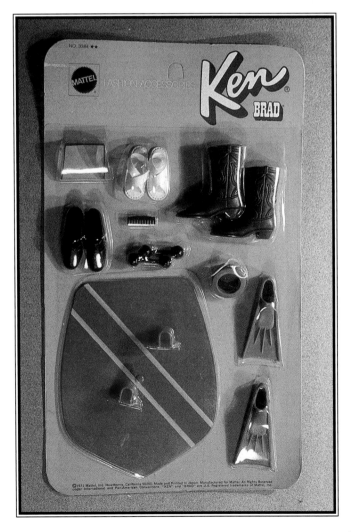

Ken Doll's
Beach Beat (1972)
#3384

The great set included a red-orange skim board with turquoise and yellow stripes; turquoise swim fins and mask; green sunglasses; black comb and bar bells; brown cowboy boots; black dress shoes; and white vinyl sandals. $125.00

Francie Doll's Looks from 1972

Busy Francie Doll
Original Outfit (1972 – 1973)
#3313

A green poor boy ribbed sleeveless top, belt, and bell bottom jeans plus green square toe shoes completed her look. Busy accessories, brown plastic TV, record player, carry case, and tray with glasses included. $50.00

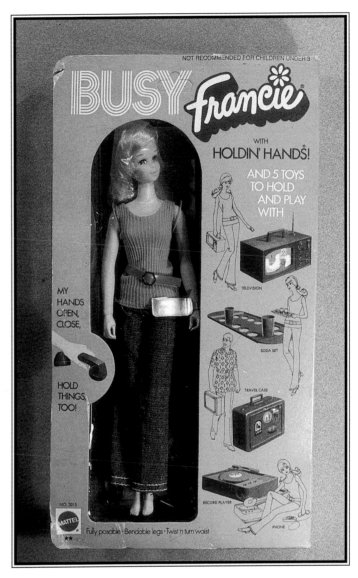

Busy Francie Doll (Germany)
Original Outfit (1972)
#3313

The Busy Francie from Germany featured a unique head mold as well as outfit! She had the usual Busy Doll's accessories, brown plastic TV, record player, carry case, and tray with glasses, but she wore a red and blue print peasant dress with navy square toe shoes. Complete with doll, $4,000.00

Francie Doll (Germany)
Original Outfit (1972)

The unique Francie doll wore a brown, linen-like mini dress with white knee-high socks and shoes. Complete with doll, $4,000.00

Francie Doll's Fashion Originals for 1972

Little Knits (1972)
#3275

Francie doll's hot pink hot pants were topped by a long sleeved print knit top with white vinyl belt. Hot pink knee socks and white vinyl sandals completed the simple but cute set. $125.00

Simply Super (1972)
#3277 (above)

This sleeveless print peasant dress featured a wide ruffle in a coordinating print at the hem and a puckered bodice. White "laced" knee-high boots completed the ensemble. $175.00

The Slacks Suit (1972)
#3276 (above)

This trendy pantsuit featured yellow, orange, and white tricot fashioned into wide leg pants and matching cropped jacket. The pants had an orange suedecloth waistband with golden buckle. The jacket featured bias cut use of the fabric for the torso and orange suede-look collar, placket, and waistband. Three goldtone bead buttons trimmed the placket and she carried a yellow vinyl shoulder bag with suedecloth and golden bead button closure. Yellow square toe shoes completed the look. $175.00

Checker Chums (1972)
#3278 (left)

Francie doll's cute mini dress featured a red tricot top and a mini check skirt and shoulder bag each with red apple appliqué. Red tricot knee socks and black flats completed the set. $175.00

Totally Terrific (1972)
#3280

This great ensemble of the '70s featured huge textured plaid for the cap and jacket. Both of these pieces had navy vinyl trim. A red tricot body blouse and yellow skirt with navy stitching, yellow tricot pantyhose, navy flats with ties, and a yellow vinyl shoulder bag with golden bead button completed the set. $225.00

Cool Casuals (1972)
#3281

Francie doll looked cute as could be in her chambray coveralls with appliqué trim on the bib. A white, lacy textured long sleeved knit top, chambray backpack with yellow vinyl straps, and yellow go-go boots completed the set ready for a day in school! $225.00

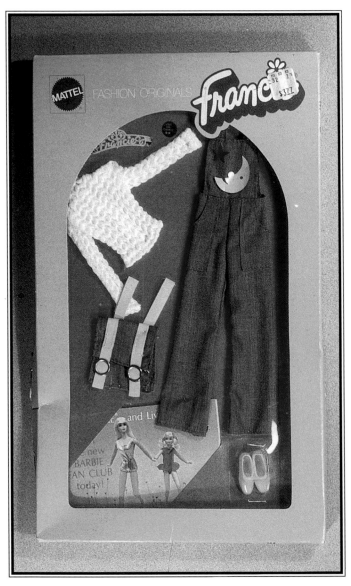

The Long View (1972)
#3282

This demure evening gown was fashioned of textured turquoise with floral braid accents on the bodice, the sleeves, and above the ruffle on the skirt's hem. Golden braid defined the empire waist and white square toe pumps completed the lovely ensemble. $225.00

Suited For Shorts (1972)
#3283

Shorts by any other name—the other name appropriate for these would be hot pants in a print that matched her sleeveless shell and stirrup knee socks. Other pieces were a zip front, red-orange mid-thigh length jacket with mid-thigh tail. A yellow vinyl shoulder bag had a golden bead and clasp. Yellow square toe shoes completed the set. $225.00

Double Ups (1972)
#3286

Lots of coordinating pieces worked together for many creative looks. The navy suedecloth was fashioned into a jacket, shoulder bag, boots, visor strap, and waistband and placket of the skirt. Red vinyl formed the bill of the visor, the straps on the boots, and the strap and tab an the shoulder bag. Big red buttons added nice detailing to the jacket and skirt. Smaller buttons accented the pocket flaps on the hot pants. A red tricot cat suit held everything together. $250.00

Peach Treats (1972)
#3285

This cool summer dress was fashioned from a pastel print and accented with an orange, ruffle-edged shawl. The empire waist dress was defined with an orange waistband and long sleeves. A full slip in cotton was trimmed at the bodice and ruffle hem with lace. The lace peeked out above the bodice and hem of the dress. Orange square toe pumps were included. $250.00

Smashin' Satin (1972)
#3287

A hard one to find as are all of these Francie doll's outfits from 1972! The pieces mixed and matched or could have been worn all together! The beautiful blue satin was accented with raspberry suedecloth. The waist-length jacket and dress had turquoise shank button detailing as did the purse, made from matching fun fur with the suedecloth. Suede-cloth trimmed hot pants, unique blue pantyhose and square toe shoes completed the set. $300.00

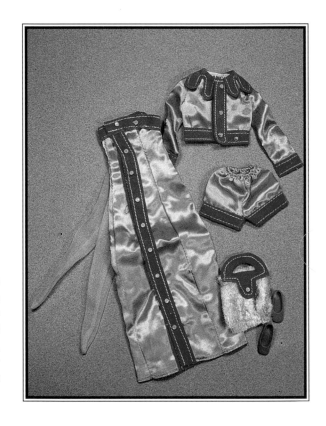

Bridal Beauty (1972)
#3288

One of the hardest to find wedding dresses was fashioned of a woven white-on-white fabric with sheer sleeves, bib ruffle, and satin ribbon neckband. The simple headpiece was a big satin bow with tulle veil. Her bouquet was a lace "basket" of yellow and blue flowers with yellow handle and white satin ribbon bow. White square toe shoes completed this desirable outfit. $500.00

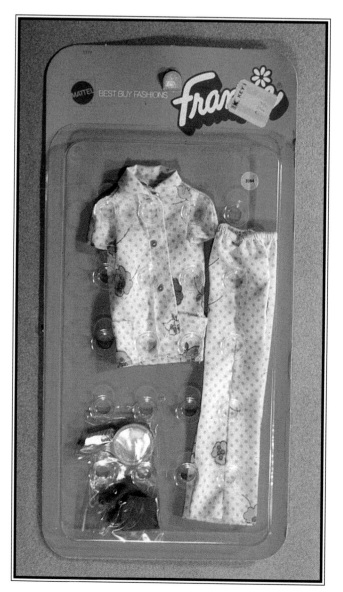

Francie Doll's Best Buy Outfits for 1972

Sleepy Time Gal (1972)
#3364

These cute tailored p.j.s coordinated with Barbie and Skipper dolls' sets. Francie doll wore a blue version of the fabric and she had blue felt booties with golden bead buttons and a blue comb, brush and mirror set. $50.00

Ready! Set! Go! (1972)
#3365

Great outfit with aqua tricot tank top and bell bottom jeans with wide brown vinyl belt with golden studs and buckle. Tennis shoes, red sunglasses, and a dots and stars print scarf completed the set. One version shown here has solid color jeans while the other set has a diagonal stripe in the jeans. $75.00

Pretty Frilly (1972)
#3366

A great little peasant dress was fashioned from a floral stripe print. The detailed bodice had a jumper look with shoulder straps with black braid edging and waist definition. The white bodice inset and puffed sleeves created the blouse look. Two black shank buttons accented the top. Black square toe shoes and a turquoise butterfly with two yellow beads on a choker necklace completed the set. $200.00

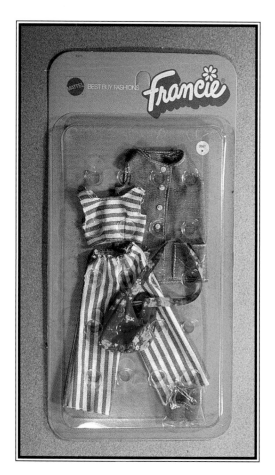

Right For Stripes (1972)
#3367

A tailored, sleeveless turquoise top had pockets and white button trim. The matching striped pedal pushers, a contrasting red floral fabric shoulder bag, and turquoise tennis shoes completed the cool summer look. Shown are two versions; one was darker and solid color, the other set featured lighter color pieces and the top had a definite diagonal stripe. $175.00

Red, White 'n Bright
(1972)
#3368 (near right)

This full length white piqué coat was detailed with a red velveteen collar, cuffs, pocket flaps, and three buttons. The red shoulder bag added another contrasting interest with golden chain and bead button. White square toe shoes completed the set. $100.00

Pink 'n Pretty (1972)
#3369 (far right)

This simple pink mini dress had eyelet trim and a hidden floral half slip and panties with lace trim. Pink square toe shoes completed the set. $100.00

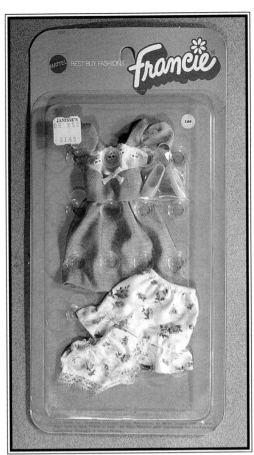

Skipper Doll's Fun Fashions from 1972

Skipper doll's fashions from 1971 were repeated and the new Pose 'n Play dolls had 10 new outfits in 1972.

Pose 'n Play
Skipper Doll
Original Outfit (1972 – 1973)
#1179 (right)

The cute doll wore a suit in blue gingham and solid tricot. Her Swing-A-Rounder gym was included with her. Suit only, $35.00

Pose 'n Play
Tiff Doll
Original Outfit (1972 – 1973)
#1199

The hard-to-find tomboy wore jeans and a white sleeveless brushed tricot top with patches. White tennis shoes and a red skateboard completed her look! Outfit only, $75.00

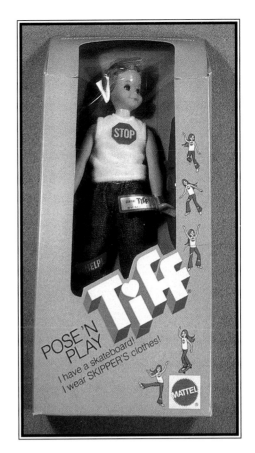

Skipper Doll's Fashion Originals for 1972

Nifty Knickers (1972)
#3291

This super outfit featured
a golden yellow, long
sleeved top with elasti-
cized waist and a red
sleeveless unique vest
stitched in yellow with two
yellow buttons. Her floral
knickers met the top of
her red knee boots.
$175.00

Play Pants (1972)
#3292

Cute denim coveralls with red vinyl straps and big red heart appliqué on
the bib topped a print shirt with red knit trim. Red knit knee highs and
white tennis shoes completed the set. $175.00

Dream Ins (1972)
#3293

This long, brushed tricot print gown featured pink nylon sheer ruffles around the yoke, hem, and sleeves and a bow at the neck. Pink felt slip-on scuffs with sheer nylon bows on top completed the set. $175.00

Turn Abouts (1972)
#3295

An incredible number of mix and match pieces were the highlights of this very '70s inspired style for Skipper doll. A print knit was fashioned into a skirt, slacks, cap with pom pon, and a sleeveless top with yellow ribbed knit waistband. Yellow ribbed shorts, a ribbed top with long red tricot sleeves with yellow cuffs, red vinyl bag with red and yellow strap, and red flat shoes completed this ensemble. $200.00

Red, White 'n Blues (1972)
#3296

Two looks in one! Skipper doll's red/white/blue mini heart print dress had solid ruffle trim and a navy tie belt. The other outfit featured a red long sleeved top with navy V neck and cuffs with white braid trim. Matching navy shorts were also trimmed in braid. Blue shoes were included and red tricot knee socks. $200.00

Party Pair (1972)
#3297

A pretty, pink velveteen party dress had a delicate white puckered fabric top and floral braid trim at the hem. A big, fluffy white fun fur coat with velveteen trim, pink pantyhose, and flats completed the very pretty set. $200.00

Skipper Doll's Best Buys Fashions for 1972

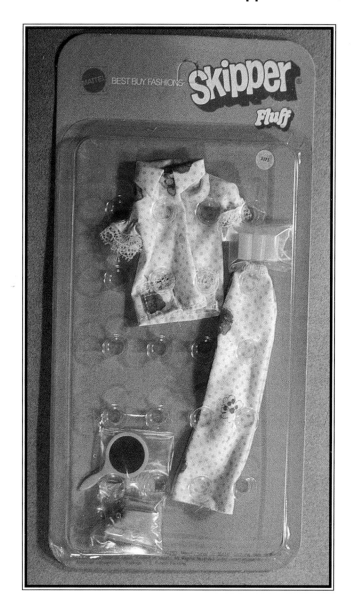

Super Snoozers (1972)
#3371

These cute tailored pajamas looked great with Barbie and Francie dolls' coordinating styles. Three, yellow plastic hair rollers, comb, brush and mirror set, and felt slippers with golden bead buttons completed the set. $50.00

Fun Runners (1972)
#3372

This casual jeans ensemble looked wonderful with Barbie doll's Good Sports #3351 and Francie doll's Ready! Set! Go! #3365. Skipper doll's yellow sleeveless tricot top and jeans were accessorized with a red vinyl belt, floral scarf, red sunglasses, and white tennis shoes. $50.00

Flower Power (1972)
#3373

Red and white, and pink and white calico formed the two skirts for this variable look. A white, puffed sleeve blouse with Peter Pan collar, three button detail, and tucking looked great with either skirt. A red tie belt with black ties and red flats completed the set. $50.00

White, Bright 'n Sparkling (1972)
#3374

Skipper doll's long, white piqué maxi coat had golden braid at the waist and golden bead buttons down the front. Her matching shoulder bag had a goldtone chain and braid trim. White flats completed the set. $50.00

Chapter VI – 1973

Give Us A Head With Hair!

When we think back to 1973, one thing that comes to mind is hair! And, hair has to be the descriptive word for the dolls of 1973. The innovative Quick Curl dolls allowed styling never before possible with so little effort. And, Ken doll got his first chance to have a REAL head of hair and some facial hair as well! What fun! In the fashion world of the Barbie doll family, the line of fully accessorized Get-Ups 'n Go outfits was launched. The Best Buy Fashion line was expanded with some of them being surprisingly interesting for the collector! And, this was the year that outfit titles were omitted and only stock numbers could identify an outfit.

Miss America doll's three outfits were repeated as was Barbie doll's shoe pak #3382. Ken doll's Sears exclusive Casual All Stars, Skipper doll's Sears exclusive Young Ideas, Francie doll's Sears exclusive Pretty Power, and Barbie doll's Sears exclusive Glamour Group, Fashion Bouquet, Accessory Pak, and Goodies Galore continued this year. Otherwise, all fashions were new!

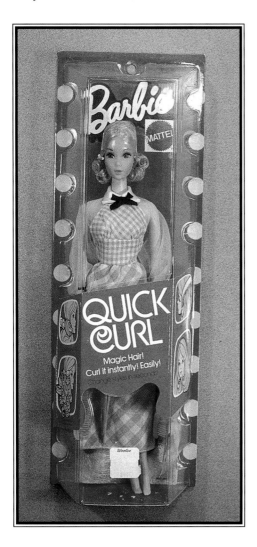

Quick Curl Barbie Doll
Original Outfit (1973 – 1975)
#4220

Pink and white gingham in two sizes and white nylon created the feminine maxi dress with prim black bow at the neck. White square toe shoes and hair accessories were included. $35.00

Baggie Non-Talk Talking
Barbie Doll
Original Outfit (1973)
#1115

Other than not talking, the doll is identical to Talking Barbie in the white vinyl two-piece swimsuit with golden cover-up. $45.00

Baggie Live Action
Barbie Doll
Original Outfit (1973)
#1155 (far right)

The same doll and outfit as the regular Live Action Barbie doll was sold in a plastic package. $45.00

Baggie Live Action
P.J. Doll
Original Outfit (1973)
#1156 (near right)

The same doll and outfit as the regular Live Action P.J. doll were sold in a plastic package. $45.00

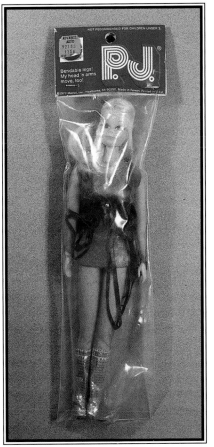
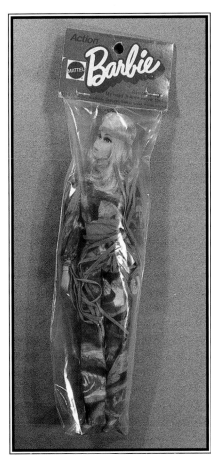

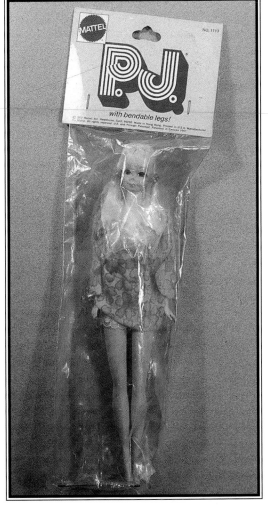

Baggie Non-Talk Talking
P.J. Doll (1973)
#1113

The non-talking doll was in her regular outfit. $45.00

Quick Curl
Miss America Doll
Original Outfit (1973 – 1976)
#8697

Although the doll's hair changed from brunette to blonde through the years, the costume remained the same with the exception of golden knit rather than lamé being used for the bodice. Quick Curl hair accessories were included. $45.00

Quick Curl Kelley Doll
Original Outfit (1973 – 1976)
#4221

Pretty green checks with dotted swiss fashioned the red-head's dress. White square toe shoes and hair accessories completed the set. $40.00

Malibu Christie Doll
Original Outfit (1973 – 1974)
#7745

The doll wore a red suit and had a white beach towel.
$25.00

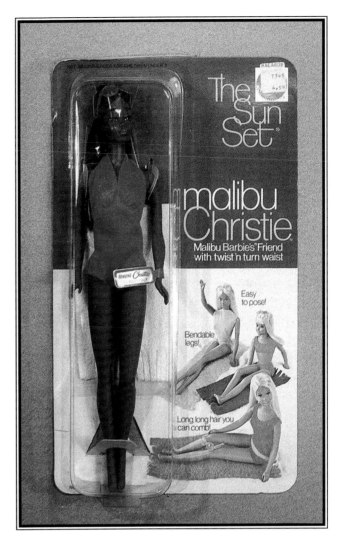

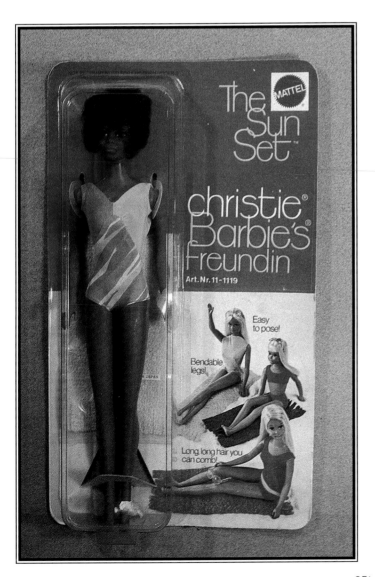

Malibu Christie (European)
Original Outfit (1973)
#1067 (on package)
#11-1119 (on attached German doll's name sticker)

The package is the same as the Malibu dolls, but the doll is Twist 'n Turn Christie doll in her appropriate swimsuit with a yellow beach towel. Outfit only, $75.00

Barbie Doll's Best Buy Fashions for 1973

#3203
(1973)

A favorite in flocked dots! The three-piece set featured a long red skirt with white dots and matching vest. The blouse coordinated in black dotted white fabric with black and white checked faille cuffs and big bow at the neck. Red chunky shoes completed the set. Shown are variations in fabric scale. $75.00

#3205
(1973)

This fresh look combined white eyelet and yellow gingham into a peasant look. The fitted blouse featured a high collar and leg-of-mutton sleeves. A yellow satin ribbon accented the waist. Her long gingham skirt ended in a ruffle at the hem. White square toe pumps completed the set. $75.00

#3206
(1973)

This great maxi dress used the fabulous fabric used in 1971's Bubbles and Boots #3421 for the big floppy hat and long skirt. The form fitting top had a high collar and a blue vinyl belt at the waist. A green satin ribbon and two orange flowers accented the hat and green square toe shoes completed the set. $65.00

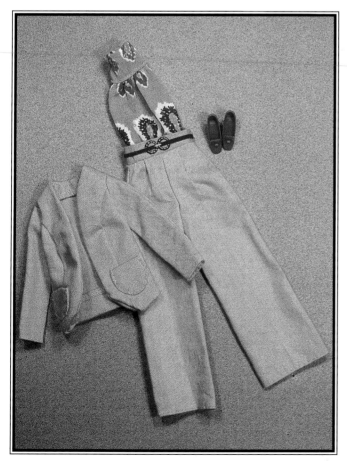

#3208
(1973)

A very nice pantsuit was fashioned in orange twill. The jacket featured rounded lines and patch pockets. A psychedelic print jersey formed the halter top of the jumpsuit. Purple shoes completed the set. $75.00

#3343
(1973)

A sweet peasant dress featured coordinating floral prints, leg-of-mutton sleeves and a big, red flower on the gros-grain ribbon belt. Red square toe shoes completed the set. $65.00

#3346
(1973)

Barbie doll went nautical in a two-piece tricot dress with dots and sailboats. A middy style collar with red braid accented the nautical print. Red square toe pumps completed the look. $55.00

#3347
(1973)

Beautiful flowers danced on this satin mini dress with A-line skirt and white collar, cuffs, and vinyl belt. White tricot socks and square toe pumps completed the set. $75.00

#3348
(1973)

Barbie doll looked as bright as the morning sun in this yellow, sheer nylon nightie lined in tricot and robe trimmed in white lace. The robe featured a yellow satin ribbon tie and the gown had yellow satin ribbon straps. $65.00

#8620
(1973)

This dress looked like two pieces with a floral ruffle hem skirt with suspenders over the white puffed sleeve bodice. A single red shank button and white lace detailed the top. Red square toe shoes completed the look. $65.00

#8621
(1973)

Blue gingham in a large scale for the skirt and sleeves was accented by a coordinating smaller gingham with sprinkles of flowers. The two-piece peasant style also featured eyelet lace trim at the neckline. White square toe shoes were included. $75.00

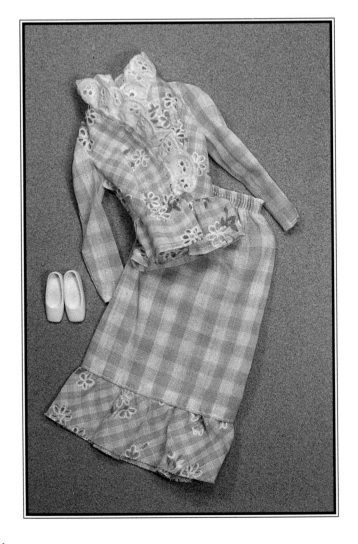

#8622
(1973)

This interesting evening ensemble used a combination of colors and textures. The white lace overblouse had an orange and a cerise flower with orange satin ribbon corsage. The sheer orange nylon skirt topped hot pink tricot pants underneath and the halter top was white tricot. The hot pink tricot formed the waistband as well. Red chunky shoes and a silvertone clutch completed the ensemble. $75.00

#8623
(1973)

Here comes the bride! This simple gown was lovely in white-on-white patterned nylon with sheer nylon sleeves, yoke, and ruffles at the yoke and at the hem. Braid accented the bodice and a ribbon formed the waistband and accented the neckline. A single white flower with green tulle spray and white satin ribbon, a headpiece with tulle veil, and white cut-out pumps completed the set. $175.00

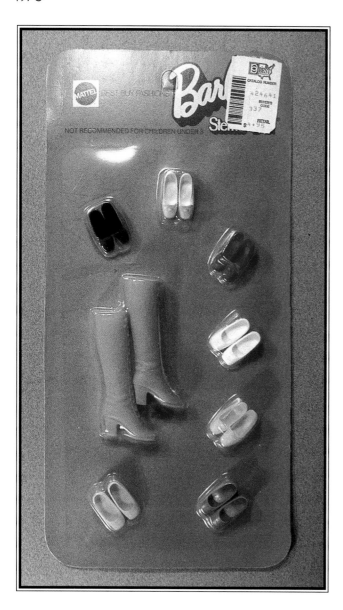

#8626
(1973 – 1974)

The set contained chunky shoes in yellow, black, white, and red; square toe pumps in white, turquoise, and pale pink; and tan "laced" knee-high boots. $65.00

#8680
(1973)

A mod print jersey formed the interest of this very simple long skirt and sleeveless, high neck halter back top. The design was interesting, with ties at the torso and the waist. Shoes completed the set. $65.00

#8681
(1973)

This set coordinated with set #8682 (following). The red and tan knit high neck sweater topped a fleece skirt with single pleat. Red square toe shoes completed the set. $65.00

#8682
(1973)

On chilly days, Barbie doll popped on her tan fleece wrap coat with matching faux fur collar. A patch pocket and tie belt added interest. Brown square toe shoes completed the set. $65.00

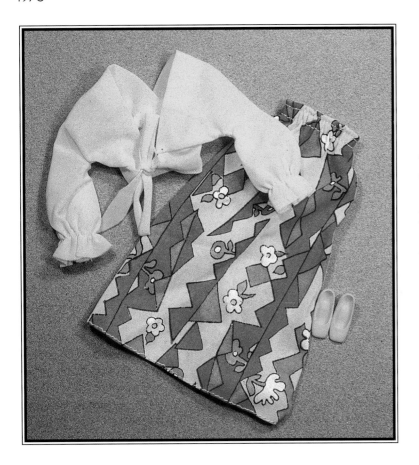

#8683
(1973)

A great, wrap-style blouse in yellow tricot topped a wild print tricot skirt. The blouse had long sleeves with gathered cuffs and a tie at the fitted waist. Yellow square toe shoes completed the fashion. $65.00

#8684
(1973)

A perfect 1973 peasant dress in unbleached muslin with natural color trim at the neckline, sleeves, and top and bottom ruffle at the hem. A single red flower accented the waistband of grosgrain ribbon. Off-white square toe shoes completed the set. $75.00

#8685
(1973)

Deceptively one piece, this jumpsuit featured printed pants with white tricot blouse and yellow sweater vest. Yellow square toe shoes completed the set. $75.00

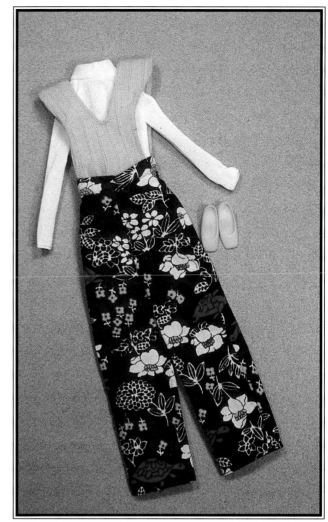

#8687
(1973)

One of my absolute favorites! This beautiful, pale pink felt pantsuit featured a big faux fur collar, tie at the waist, and patch pockets. The pink tricot blouse was backless and was held on by Barbie doll's arms going through straps. White square toe shoes completed the set. $100.00

#8688
(1973)

This pink, halter gown with black flocked dot overskirt and shawl was accented by a velvet waistband with a huge white flower. Pink square toe shoes completed the set. $65.00

#8689
(1973)

The sheer tricot blouse had sheer nylon sleeves and was accented with lace. Barbie doll's satin skirt had a hem ruffle and two flowers and a bow accent at the waistband. White square toe shoes completed the set. Color variations are shown. $75.00

#8690
(1973)

Barbie doll's lovely, full-length white gown with pink nylon bodice and bow was topped by a pretty floral satin robe with pink nylon ruffles and a pink bow at the neck. $75.00

#8691
(1973)

This great-looking ensemble was very versatile with a white fitted blouse with big red flower on the collar and red vinyl belt that topped either skirt or pants in a red fabric with white dots. An open crown nylon circular hat was piped in the dotted fabric and she had red square toe shoes as accessories. $75.00

#8692
(1973)

This peasant inspired gown was fashioned in blue satin. Lace at the high neck and around the sheer yoke added a quaint appeal. A lavender satin ribbon accented the waist and high neck. Two flowers accented the waist. Blue chunky shoes completed the ensemble. $75.00

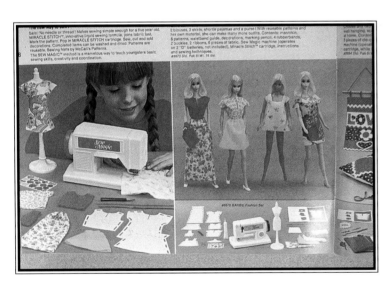

Sew Magic Barbie Doll Fashion Set
#8670
(1973 – 1975)

The Sew Magic set contained the makings for four Barbie doll outfits. The pieces were a dress, two blouses, two skirts, shorty pajamas, and a purse. The set contained reusable patterns, notions, and fabric as well as the machine, mannequin, and more accessories. Complete set, $100.00

Barbie And Ken Dolls' Fashions
#7726
(1973 – 1974)

There was a Sew Magic Add Ons kit which featured Ken doll's swim trunks; sleeveless shirt and pants; shirt; pants; vest; swim trunks and shorts; suit and wild shirt; and pants. For Barbie doll, long dress; poncho and slacks; feminine long dress; shorts; and top. $55.00

Get-Ups 'n Go

A new line of clothing that featured more detail and accessories than the more economical Best Buys with more elaborate packaging as well.

#7700
(1973 – 1976)

The very first time Barbie doll became a doctor was 1973 with this outfit! She had the blue surgical smock, head covering, and mask as well as her white doctor's coat. Accessories were a stethoscope; head mirror; diploma; skeletal chart; blue towel; princess phone (samples here show phone in red or blue); and white square toe shoes. $75.00

#7701
(1973 – 1974)

Barbie doll, the ballerina, practiced in a long sleeved black leotard with sheer black tights (same as pantyhose). She performed in a white satin ballet costume with golden glinted net tutu. The satin bodice was trimmed with gold and white braid. Pink ballet shoes, pink satin toe shoe bag, Ballet Company announcement, a gold foil flexible tiara, and two silk roses completed the set. This outfit coordinated with Skipper doll's set #7714. $75.00

#7702
(1973 – 1974)

Barbie doll was ready for a camping trip in her light blue denim slacks with matching backpack and red plaid fleece shirt with large golden bead button at the waist and a red shell. She wore red tennis shoes and had her own green calico and red flannel sleeping bag. Her outfit coordinated with Ken doll's #7706 and Skipper doll's #7715 Get-Ups 'n Go outfits. $65.00

#7703
(1973 – 1975)

The third airline Barbie doll flew with was United! Her uniform consisted of mix and match pieces: a red skirt; navy slacks; navy vest; dotted body blouse with tie at the neck; a red top with striped sleeves and high neck; and a navy vinyl belt. Navy square toe shoes completed the set. Ken doll was her Captain in his Get-Ups 'n Go outfit #7707. $75.00

Ken Doll's Looks for 1973

Baggie Non-Talk Talking Ken Doll
Original Outfit (1973)
#1111

Dressed in the second Talking Ken doll's outfit, this Ken doll had no talking pull cord. $40.00

Mod Hair
Ken Doll
(1973 – 1976)
#4224

How marvelous! A Ken doll with real hair! His original outfit consisted of a big plaid jacket that started off as a woven fabric and later in the run, a printed check was used. There were lots of variation in the scale of the checks as well. He also wore brown slacks and shoes. $35.00

Baggie Live Action
Ken Doll
Original Outfit (1973)
#1159

This was the same doll as the one in the Live Action and Live Action On Stage series. $45.00

Ken Doll's Best Buy Fashions for 1973

#8615 (right)
(1973)

This crisp summery outfit consisted of white slacks with contrasting red top stitching and big cargo pockets. He teamed them with a red print long sleeved shirt with white collar and cuffs. White tennis shoes completed the set. $50.00

#8616 (above)
(1973)

Ken doll's number was 73 in 1973! He wore this winning navy and gold knit shirt with a big red felt 73 and navy vinyl belt with navy slacks and black shoes. $50.00

#8617
(1973)

This Western inspired suit was made of beige suede-cloth with sherpa-look trim on the jacket. The slacks matched and Ken doll coordinated the suit with a gold turtleneck dickie and brown shoes. $65.00

#8618
(1973)

Ken doll's mod suit for 1973 was fashioned of blue flannel and had red plaid collar and cuffs, plus red buttons. A red three corner tricot scarf and black shoes completed the set. $50.00

#8627
(1973 – 1974)

Ken doll's shoe pak contained two pairs of cowboy boots in tan and black; tennis shoes in white, blue, and brown, each with white painted soles; dress shoes in brown, white, and black. $75.00

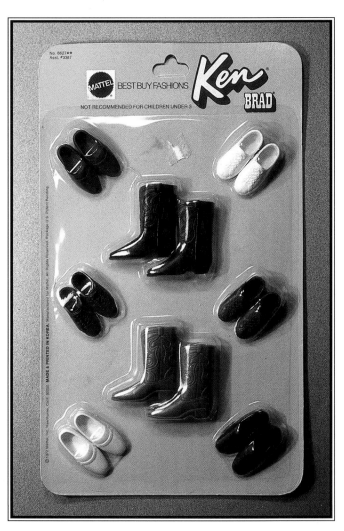

Ken Doll's Get-Ups 'n Go Outfits for 1973

#7705
(1973)

Dr. Ken doll had an outfit that coordinated with Barbie doll's Get-Ups 'n Go outfit #7700. He also had the blue surgeon's top, head covering, and mask as well as his white slacks and doctor's coat. His accessories were a stethoscope, head mirror, and white shoes. $75.00

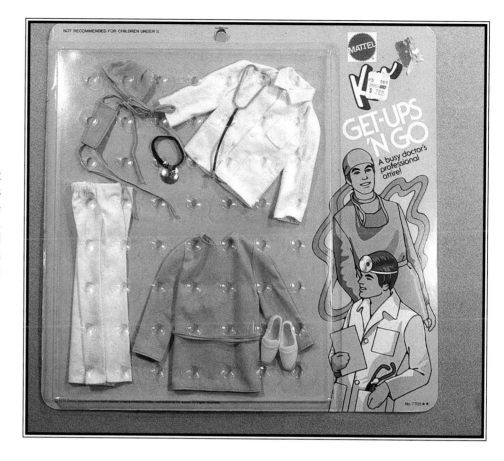

#7706
(1973 – 1974)

Ken doll's camping set coordinated with Barbie doll's Get-Ups 'n Go outfit #7702 and Skipper doll's #7715. He wore a neat tan safari type shirt with four patch pockets and brown shank buttons with a brown vinyl belt with two golden bead buttons as the closure rather than a buckle. He had matching brown elastic-back slacks and carried a brown vinyl backpack. He wore a yellow tricot neck scarf, brown cowboy boots, and had a masculine brown plaid flannel and pale orange sleeping bag. $65.00

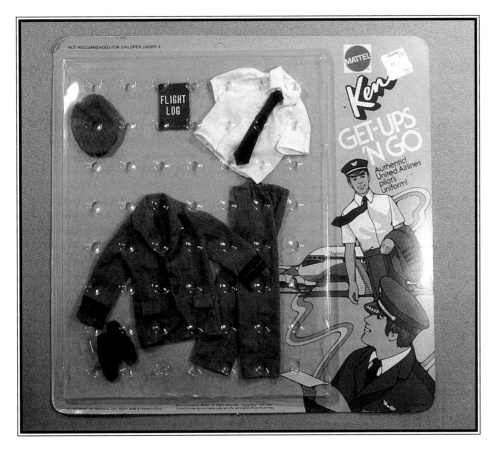

#7707
(1973 – 1975)

Ken doll made the most handsome pilot in his blue United Airline's pilot uniform! He had four black stripes on the sleeves and black buttons at the jacket front. His pilot's wings decorated his chest. He wore matching slacks with a white shirt, black tie and pilot's cap with black vinyl bill and golden ornamentation. Black shoes completed the look. He also had his flight log which looked like the one from American Airlines Captain #0779 from 1964 – 1965 but this newer version was marked Korea, not Japan. See the variation in fabrics used in the photo. $75.00

Francie Doll's Fun Looks for 1973!

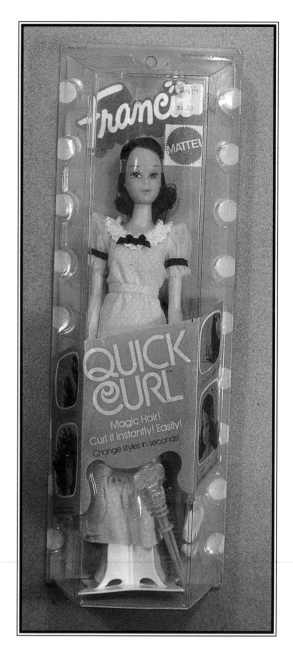

Quick Curl
Francie Doll
Original Outfit (1973 – 1974)
#4222

Francie doll's dress was a bit more youthful in design than Quick Curl Barbie doll's. The bright yellow and white dress was accented with white nylon and a black bow at the neck. White square toe shoes and her Quick Curl hair accessories completed the set. $35.00

Francie Doll's Best Buy Fashions from 1973

#8644
(1973)

Patriotic red/white/blue sundress featured tiny blue gingham with red braid on the halter top and waist. Eyelet and red fabric with blue dots formed the two ruffles at the hem. $50.00

#8645
(1973)

Francie doll looked great in this cute mini dress of flower sprinkled burgundy gingham. A white tricot collar and red vinyl belt added to the crisp look. White tricot knee socks completed the set. $50.00

#8646
(1973)

Francie doll's brown flannel coat coordinated with the dress #8647 following. The coat had a white fun fur collar, two goldtone button trim, and vinyl belt. A flannel cap with vinyl bill completed the set. $50.00

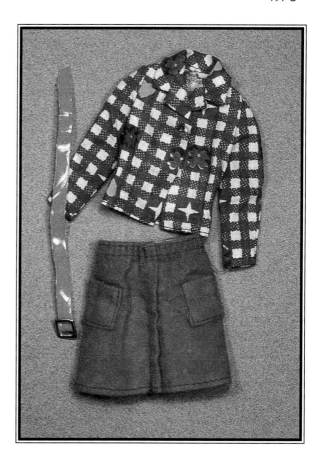

#8647 (right)
(1973)

The perfect partner for the previous coat was this outfit which featured a flower sprinkled, brown gingham long sleeved top with flannel skirt. A pink vinyl belt added contrast and picked up the color of some of the flowers. $50.00

#8648 (above)
(1973)

This year's cute sleepwear set featured bright peach sheer nylon in a short gown and robe set. The gown was lined in tricot. White lace accented the square yokes of the gown and the robe. A ribbon tied at the neck of the robe. $50.00

#8649 (right)
(1973)

This casual set featured red, anchor print slacks with yellow rickrack. The top was a combination of three fabrics: a red collar with anchors, solid yellow yoke, and navy anchor print body with yellow rickrack trim. A single shank button accented the neckline. $50.00

#8625
(1973 – 1974)

Francie doll's shoe pak included brown "laced" knee boots; square toe shoes in yellow, green, black, white, pink, orange, blue; and white tennis shoes. $50.00

Francie Doll's Get-Ups 'n Go Outfits for 1973

#7709
(1973)

Francie doll made a cute Candy Striper in her pink striped jumper over a white blouse with collar and short sleeves. She wore a solid white and pink striped nurse's cap and white square toe shoes. Her accessories were numerous: a blue tray with orange juice; bouquet of red and purple flowers; a yellow brushed tricot blanket with satin binding at the top and bottom; a hot water bottle; soap; pillow; and blue terry wash cloth. $100.00

#7710
(1973 – 1975)

Francie doll's great beach set included a two-piece swimsuit in navy and white checked jersey. Her beach dress was fashioned of the same fabric with yellow trim and vinyl flower appliques. Her accessories were yellow swim mask; snorkel; swim fins; blue sunglasses; yellow terry towel; and skim board. $75.00

#7711
(1973 – 1975)

What a great little cheerleader Francie doll made in her outfit that featured a red and white knit top with white felt "M" and pleated tricot skirt, all in one piece! She wore jersey tights, a red knit cap, and white "laced" knee-high boots. Her finishing touches were two red crepe paper pom pons, a white plastic megaphone with red painted trim, and a paper "Go Team" pennant on a wooden stick with vinyl handle. $75.00

Skipper Doll's Fashions for 1973

Baggie
Skipper Doll (1973)
#1117

This was the same doll as Pose 'n Play Skipper doll #1179. She came in both ash blonde and light blonde. $35.00

Quick Curl
Skipper Doll
Original Outfit (1973 – 1975)
#4223

This cutie wore a blue gingham and solid color maxi dress with a ribbon in her hair and white flats. She had all the Quick Curl hair accessories, too. $35.00

Skipper Doll (European) (1973)
#8519

The pretty doll wore a pretty swimsuit in blue with pink
and white flowers. The wrap design with accent bow and
pleated ruffle in white had contrasting hot pink panties.
Complete set, $1,000.00

Skipper Doll's Best Buy Fashions from 1973

#8610
(1973)

Skipper doll looked so cute in her bright yellow maxi
dress with pink and blue rickrack trim and white
blouse look on the bodice. $50.00

#8611 (left)
(1973)

Skipper doll's cute dress looked ready for school. The two pieces looked like three with a red knit vest over a jersey dress with white blouse and a navy floral skirt. The blouse was stitched in navy and she had a navy tie at the neck. White jersey knee socks and red flats completed the ensemble. $45.00

#8612 (right)
(1973)

This cute nightie set included a pink floral flannel wrap robe with pink tricot trim and a self tie. The matching tricot nightie had lace and two of the tiniest "pearl" buttons at the yoke! $45.00

#8613 (left)
(1973)

Ready for winter's chill, Skipper doll wore a red flannel coat with white fun fur collar and hem trim. A red vinyl belt and a hat that matched the coat completed the set. $50.00

Skipper Doll's Get-Ups 'n Go Outfits for 1973

Get-Ups 'n Go outfits apply only to top left and bottom photos on this page.

#7713
(1973 – 1974)

This was a great pajama party set for Skipper doll! Her two piece pajamas featured footed p.j. bottoms and an eyelet trimmed top. She wore a chartreuse night cap with eyelet trim. She had a matching sleeping bag, pink hair rollers, chartreuse comb, brush, and mirror, plus a white furry cat with hot pink neck ribbon. $65.00

#8624
(1973 – 1975)

Skipper doll's shoe pak included four hangers; and flats in royal, burgundy, orange, forest green, black, white, hot pink, and yellow. $75.00

#7714 (left)
(1973 – 1974)

Skipper doll's cute ballet outfit coordinated nicely with big sis Barbie doll's set #7701. Skipper doll wore pale pink tights and leotard, a rose colored coverup or a white satin ballet outfit with white tulle and silvery net tutu and silvery braid trim. She also had pink toe shoes, a satin toe shoe bag, and comb and brush. $75.00

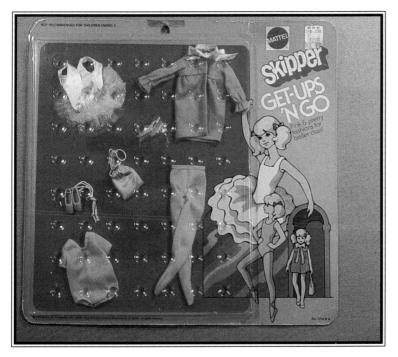

#7715
(1973)

Ready to go camping with Barbie doll in #7702 and Ken doll in #7706, Skipper doll wore a blue chambray shorts outfit with matching jacket and a brown print shirt. She had a red hat, brown vinyl back pack, blue knit knee-high socks, and white tennis shoes. Her sleeping bag was fashioned from orange flannel and blue striped fabric. $65.00

Sew Magic Add Ons
Francie And Skipper Dolls' Fashions
(1973)
#7727

The set contained the supplies needed to make Francie doll a poncho set; shorty pajamas; a long dress; shorts and shirt; and a mini dress. For Skipper doll, a school look outfit; playsuit; nightie; dress and hat; and a poncho set. $55.00

Chapter VII – 1974

Barbie Doll Is Sweet 16!

Barbie doll hit this monumental milestone as the last "birthday" she would celebrate! The following celebrations of her longevity have been referred to as "anniversaries!" The Sweet 16 Barbie doll had a sweet look of innocence almost to the point of a vacant countenance.

Besides a birthday to celebrate, the dolls for 1974 were a salute to sports and physical activity. The Sports Set dolls camped, sailed, and skied their way into the hearts of little girls. Their clothing was still influenced by economics and the less elaborate, less expensive Best Buy Fashions prevailed, but matching outfits for the dolls added interest to the collection. The Get-Ups 'n Go outfits continued with new styles added. And some of the most exciting aspects of 1974 were the dolls and outfits available in other countries, including Tutti and Todd dolls and their friend Chris doll!

In repeats, there were few items that were continued in the clothing line; some of the shoe paks were, such as Barbie doll's #8626.

Barbie Doll Sweet 16 Promo Set
Original Outfit (1974 – 1975)
#7796

The innocent lass was dressed in a demure pink and white dotted swiss dress but she also had a more casual look in jeans shorts and a yellow tank top with her Sweet 16 logo. White square toe shoes completed the ensemble. After this introductory set, the doll came without the extra casual outfit. $45.00

Sun Valley
Barbie Doll
Original Outfit (1974 – 1976)
#7806

The yellow and orange nylon jumpsuit had a matching jacket. She had ski poles, skis, and mask for skiing. $45.00

Newport Barbie Doll
Original Outfit (1974 – 1975)
#7807

In red trimmed two-piece white pantsuit or two-piece striped swimsuit, Barbie doll was ready for the ocean. She had sailing accessories, too. $45.00

Baggie Babs Doll (1974)
#7888

More significant than realized, this doll was identical to the Busy Steffie doll, however she established a new character in the Barbie doll family tree! This was the one and only appearance of Babs doll in the Barbie doll family. $45.00

Malibu
P.J. Doll
Original Outfit (1974)
#1187

The Taiwan version featured a green (not lavender) swimsuit for this doll! She was much harder to find than the one in the more common lavender suit. $75.00

Yellowstone
Kelley Doll
Original Outfit (1974)
#7808

Always a hard-to-find doll, the cute redhead wore either her blue and white camping shorts or pants with a red and white dotted shirt. She had knee-high tricot socks and tennis shoes. $65.00

Sears Exclusive
Barbie Doll Babysits (1974 – 1976)
#7882

The adorable new character in the Barbie doll family had lots of plastic play pieces as well as a sacque, bunting, christening gown and bonnet, plus an apron for Barbie doll. $65.00

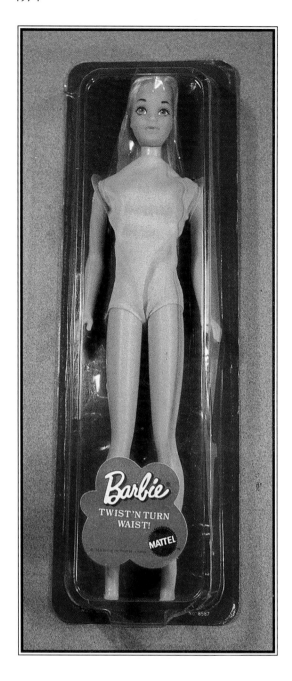

Barbie Doll (Canada, Germany and Italy)
(1974)
#8587

The doll from Canada wore a yellow, one-piece tricot swimsuit as shown at the left. #8587 from Germany wore a blue swimsuit (not shown) identical to that of Malibu Barbie doll. The doll from Italy (below) had red hair and also wore the Malibu suit. Yellow $45.00. Blue $25.00

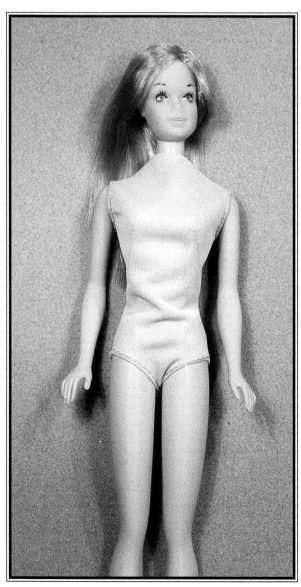

Barbie Doll (Europe)
(1974)
#8588

The doll with two ponytails wore a halter style, one-piece hot pink tricot swimsuit. $45.00

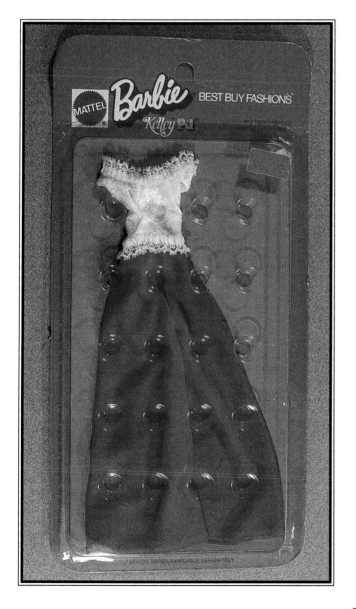

Barbie Doll Best Buy Fashions for 1974

#7746
(1974)

Barbie doll's pretty red tricot palazzo pants were topped by a white lace-over-tricot bodice trimmed in double lace around the neckline and at the waist. $45.00

#7747
(1974)

This summery two-piece set featured white flower appliqués scattered on the top with gathered waist skirt. Braid formed the straps and trimmed the skirt above the ruffled hem. $50.00

#7748
(1974)

Barbie doll's two-piece suit was fashioned of a red calico print with white lace on the sleeves. The lacy front was formed by a dickie. $45.00

#7750 (left)
(1974)

This neat and tidy two-piece set was fashioned from a blue geometric print and had white detailing, two red shank buttons, black neck tie, and white vinyl belt. This outfit coordinated with Skipper doll's #7772 Best Buy outfit. $65.00

#7749 (above)
(1974)

Icy blue looked great on one of this year's suntanned dolls! The blue sleeveless long dress had a ruffle at the hem and a knee-length white apron trimmed with lace and rickrack. $65.00

#7751
(1974)

This Hawaiian print coordinated with Skipper doll's #7771 and Ken doll's #3387. Barbie doll's halter top matched the patches on her jeans. The patches were included for the child to attach to the jeans. $65.00

#7752
(1974)

Quite a lovely three-piece suit in turquoise. The sweater had a big white collar and was reminiscent of Mood For Music #940. There was a matching shell and A-line skirt with golden chain belt and two patch pockets in front. $100.00

#7753
(1974)

Barbie doll wore this three-piece set for special occasions. The brown fleece formed the long skirt which was topped by a gold knit shell and a faux fur front fleece jacket with buckle at the waist. $100.00

#7754
(1974)

This pretty tailored pink shorty satin gown had a placket front with two shank buttons, lace trim, and nylon tie at the neck. She topped it off with a long terry robe with satin trim and tie belt. $65.00

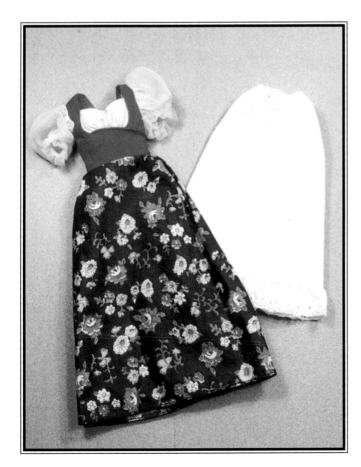

#7755
(1974)

Barbie doll's peasant look calico print coordinated with Skipper doll's #7773 and Francie doll's #7769. This pretty dress had sheer sleeves with red vest look with the navy print skirt. A long white slip with eyelet hem ruffle completed the set. $65.00

1974

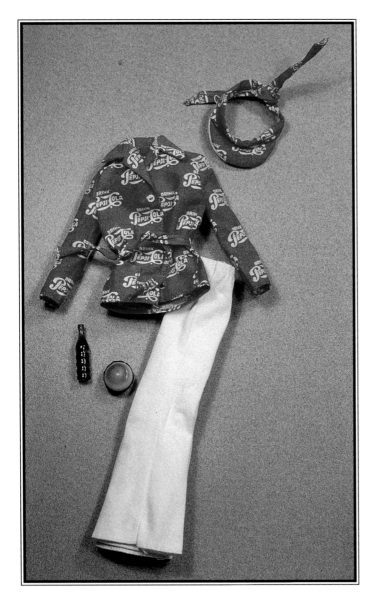

#7756
(1974)

The Pepsi generation was the first line of clothing tied to a product or a company other than the airline uniforms. The red cloth with white Pepsi logo print in white was used on coordinating outfits for Skipper doll's #7770, Francie doll's #7766 and Ken doll's #7761. Barbie doll's outfit featured a Pepsi print shirt with tie belt worn over white pants with a red sun hat. A plastic hamburger and a brown bottle (no logo but we know it is supposed to be a Pepsi!) were also included. $95.00

#7757
(1974)

Barbie doll dressed up in in a long, red crepe dress with rose sheer nylon ruffles as accents on the long sleeves and down the front. Two pink flowers with nylon ruffle formed a corsage on her shoulder. $65.00

#7813
(1974)

This outfit was simple but looked very nice on a doll. The red with white dots tricot formed the halter top with gathered waist and wide leg pants. $50.00

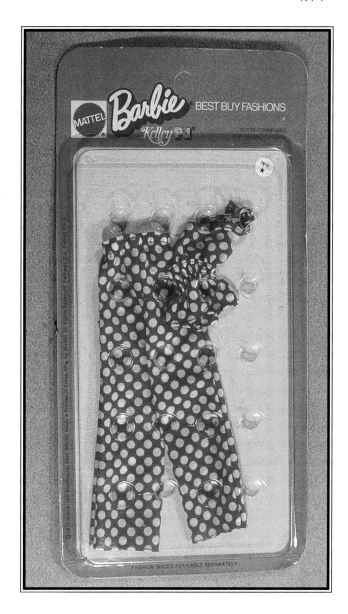

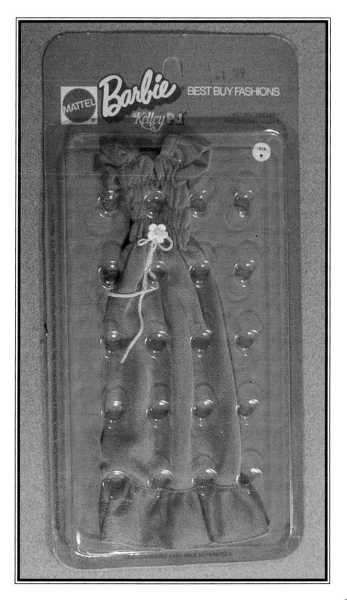

#7814
(1974)

Bright orange tricot was gathered for the bodice, flutter sleeves, and long skirt with a ruffle. It looked fresh on Sweet 16 Barbie doll. A flower and yellow cord accented the waist. $50.00

#7816 (right)
(1974)

This cute shorty nightie was fashioned from lots of hot pink sheer nylon over tricot. A double ruffle accented the neckline and down the front. A self bow accented the empire waist. Matching panties were included. $50.00

#7815 (above)
(1974)

The colorful plaid of this fabric added interest to this simple suit with big white collar. The waists of both the jacket and the matching skirt were elasticized. A single large red button at the waist accented the jacket. $75.00

#7817 (right)
(1974)

Barbie doll stayed cool in this bright red hat! It looked great with her halter dress with striped waistband and short skirt. $50.00

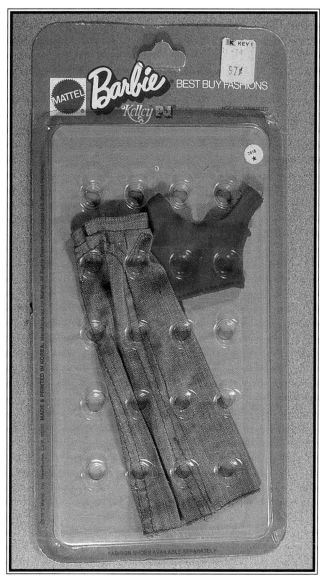

#7818
(1974)

Barbie doll's set included a red knit tank and blue chambray jeans with red stitching. $50.00

#7819
(1974)

This blue chambray midi coat had lots of interest with red shank buttons, stitching, and self belt with round goldtone buckle. A red and white dotted three corner scarf completed the set. $65.00

#7820
(1974)

This evening ensemble in fiery red included a long gown topped by a matching nylon jacket with sheer sleeves tied at the waist with ecru satin ribbon. Ecru lace trimmed both the gown and jacket. A white comb and brush completed the set. $65.00

#7821
(1974)

Barbie doll's business look was updated with a red and cream plaid fabric. The dress had a cream bodice with red shank buttons and stitching. A red hat that fades to tan even NRFB completed the look. $75.00

#7822
(1974)

Orange and blue looked great in this unique set. The jacket featured blue shank buttons and stitching over blue pants. The hat matched the jacket and had a clear vinyl brim. $85.00

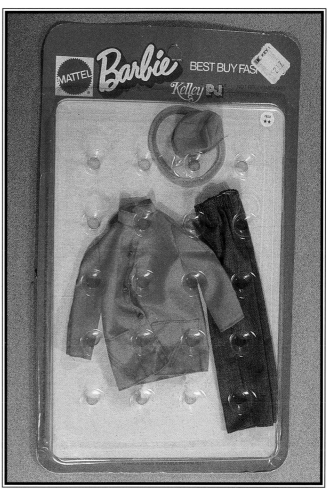

#7823
(1974)

This mix and match outfit had blue chambray shorts, A-line skirt, and bag stitched in red. The red and white striped tricot blouse had a red elastic waistband. A red scarf with white dots was tucked into her bag. $75.00

#7824
(1974)

This pretty peasant look featured off white and soft turquoise rickrack. The dress had lace sleeves that matched the apron and bodice inset. $75.00

Barbie Doll's Get-Ups 'n Go Outfits for 1974

All four of last year's sets were repeated this year and seven new ones were added.

Skiing (1974)
#7787

Barbie doll was ready for the slopes in her red and white checkerboard print stiff nylon jacket with ribbed collar, cuffs, and waistband over matching red nylon ski pants. She had a red brushed nylon cap, mittens, white ski boots, blue skis, and ski poles with blue accents. $75.00

Beach (1974)
#7788

A pretty bright floral print in red, white, and yellow tricot formed the mix and match pieces. The two-piece swimsuit featured a tie accent on the top. A sleeveless bodice with white sailor collar with red ribbon as trim and long skirt had a self belt with yellow buckle plus yellow swim fins, snorkel, face mask, and red with stenciled floral design skim board. $75.00

Bride (1974)
#7839

Barbie doll's new wedding dress for 1974 was fashioned of white lightweight but stiff satin with nylon ruffles at the neck, yoke, and hem. The same textured nylon formed the long sleeves. A satin headpiece had a tulle veil. She carried a bouquet of three white flowers with yellow tulle and she wore white square toe shoes. This ensemble coordinated with Ken doll's Get-Ups 'n Go Bridegroom #7836 and Skipper doll's Get-Ups 'n Go Flower Girl #7847. $100.00

Party Dress (1974)
#7840

This stiff satin brocade dress featured a turquoise satin halter top with red flower accent and matching jacket with white faux fur collar. Turquoise accented the ensemble as a closure with goldtone buckle on the jacket and for her clutch bag. Turquoise open toe pumps completed the ensemble that was fashioned from the same fabric used in Ken doll's Bridegroom #7836. $100.00

Party Separates (1974)
#7841

Five pieces coordinated into lots of different evening looks! The stiff hot pink satin created the bra top, long pants, A-line short skirt, and the wrap tie jacket with pink and silver floral lamé collar. A lamé long skirt and pink open toe pumps completed the lovely ensemble. $100.00

Tennis (1974)
#7842

Barbie doll was ready for the courts in her crisp red, white, and blue tennis ensemble. She wore a tennis dress with short jacket over matching panties. Her tote bag and sun visor featured red fabric with white polka dots. The visor had a clear vinyl bill. The bag held her gray plastic racquet and yellow tennis ball. White knit socks and tennis shoes completed the winning set. $75.00

Party Dress (1974)
#7843

This was a pretty set that featured a dress with tangerine satin skirt, gold lamé waistband, and lamé top. The brocade fabric was like that found in Silver Blues #3357 and Fancy That Purple #3362 from 1972. Soft gold knit accented the lamé jacket front and tied at the waist. A tan faux fur stole backed in tangerine satin, a golden clutch and orange square toe pumps completed the set. $100.00

Sew Magic Outfits from 1974

Barbie Doll's Sweet 16 Fashions (1974)
#7850

The makings for a short dress; a two-piece suit; and a long dress trimmed in faux fur were included in this set. $55.00

Knit Magic (1974)
#7830

The machine came with the makings for a halter dress and furry hat. Complete set, $100.00

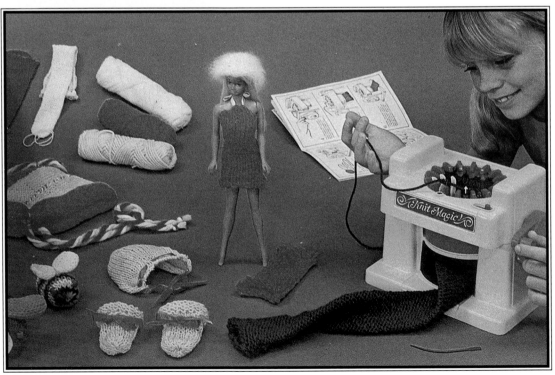

Sears Exclusive
Barbie Doll Outfit
1974

The exclusive set included long red print and
solid yellow peasant dress with black braid and
ribbon trim; a white halter top; a two-piece knit
suit with floral blouse with a black tie at the
neck; denim jeans and jacket; and white knit halter. $150.00

Sears Exclusive
Barbie Doll Outfit (1974)

This set included a long green, navy, and red print
peasant dress, pink nightie and print robe, and a
brown fleece and fun fur coat and hat with matching vinyl belt. $150.00

Sears Exclusive
Barbie Doll Outfit (1974)

A very lovely red evening gown and jacket featured white
faux fur on the jacket. Red chunky shoes, a white flower on
red choker, red princess phone, and corsage completed the
set. $150.00

Sears Exclusive
Barbie Doll Sweet 16 Outfit (1974)

Red, white, and blue pieces mix and match for lots of great looks as shown on the package! In red and white double checked fabric: blazer with pink flower on the lapel and single large white button at the placket; flared leg pants; halter top; skirt. White pieces were: tricot sleeveless blouse with collar; shorts; skirt; and slacks. In chambray were: a sleeveless blouse with collar; long skirt; and white tricot shawl with chambray ruffle. $150.00

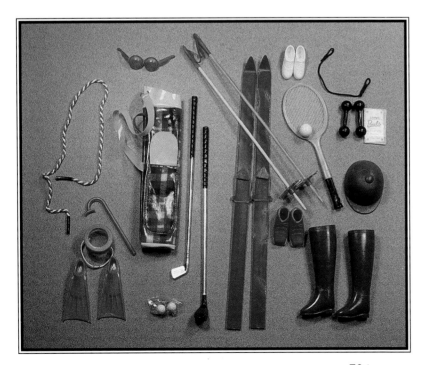

Sears Exclusive
Barbie Doll Sports Goodies
(1974)

The set included plaid golf bag; two clubs; balls; orange swim fins; snorkel; face mask; tennis racquet; ball; tennis shoes; exercise manual; exercise cord; bar bells; jump rope; pink skis; ski poles; ski boots; riding boots; riding cap; and blue sunglasses. $150.00

Barbie Doll Outfits from Other Countries

There were six mix and match pieces and seven complete ensembles available in Europe that were not available in the U.S. in 1974.

Some of the mix and match pieces featured familiar fabrics. They were blue shorts; red straight skirt; blue pants; floral long sleeved blouse; dotted blouse; and two pairs of sheer yellow panties with lace. $75.00 each

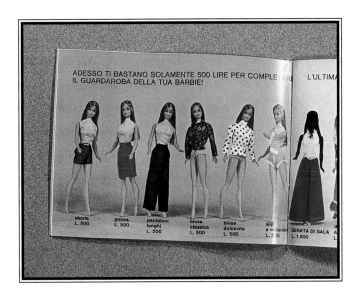

Mix 'n Match Fashions (European)
(1974)
#7988

Shown are some of the paks available for mixing and matching in Europe. $75.00 each

Tanti Pois
(1974)

Bright dots and solids formed this ensemble of two looks in one. The print dress had a red hat, blue vinyl purse, and red chunky shoes as accessories. Also included were print palazzo pants, red top, and blue vinyl belt. $250.00

Party Elegante
(1974)

Floral lamé (seen in this year's Get-Ups 'n Go #7843, 1972's Silver Blues #3357 and Fancy That Purple #3362) formed the wide leg evening pantsuit with orange satin jacket and purse. Orange shoes completed the set. $250.00

Moda Maglia
(1974)

This evening ensemble was the direct pattern of Important In-Vestment #1482 with long sleeved heavy weave turquoise dress with chain belt and faux fur vest with accent red flowers. Also included were a print hat, purse and shoes. $250.00

Prime Pioggie
(1974)

Interesting mix and match pieces in orange, yellow, and white houndstooth knit with solid yellow knit and solid orange. The houndstooth was used for a skirt and pants while the orange formed the blouse. A yellow knit coat had goldtone bead buttons. Yellow knee boots completed the set. $250.00

Coordinato Giovanne
(1974)
The 1974 jacket dress was red with blue bodice, four goldtone bead buttons at the empire waist; striped tank top and blue slacks; red hose and shoes completed the combo. $250.00

Pelliccia Sportiva
(1974)
Great looking coordinates in brown featured pieces similar to our Suede 'n Fur #3491 from 1972. The coat was part faux fur and topped a buttoned skirt and top. Matching hat, bag, and knee-high boots completed the stylish look. (The U.S. version had no hat.) $250.00

Primi Freddi
(1974)
This pink jumpsuit was topped with a faux fur vest with three rows of braid. Accessories were a faux fur bag, pink turban, and shoes. This set was similar to our Wild Things #3439 from 1971. $250.00

Ken Doll Active Looks for 1974

Baggie Non Talking
Action Ken Doll
Original Outfit (1974)
#1159

The doll had the talking Ken doll body, the Live Action Ken doll head, and the blue and orange beach set of the second Talking Ken doll. $45.00

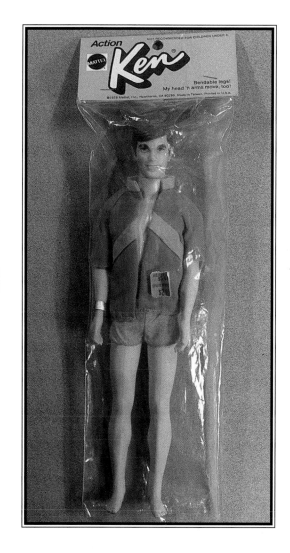

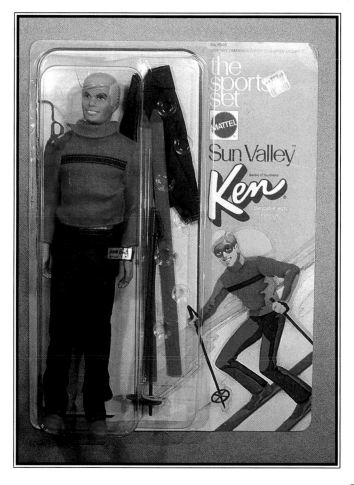

Sun Valley
Ken Doll
Original Outfit (1974 – 1975)
#7809

Perfect with Sun Valley Barbie doll, Ken doll was ready to ski in a blue nylon set with red knit top. Red boots and goggles plus blue poles completed the look. $50.00

Montgomery Ward Exclusive
Dressed Mod Hair Ken Doll (1974 – 1976)
#4234

The regular Mod Hair Ken doll came with red trunks as well as the Get-Ups 'n Go Bridegroom #7836 in a brown box. Complete, $175.00

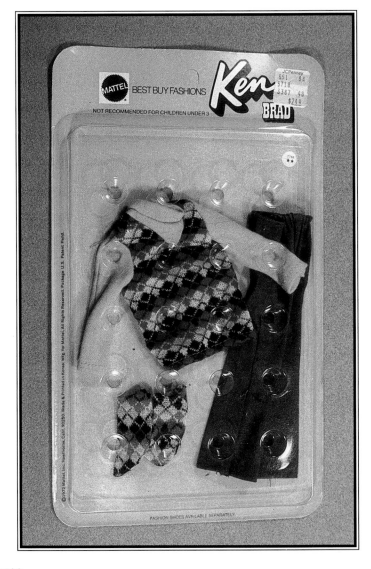

Ken Doll's Best Buy Fashions for 1974

Ken doll had quite a few new looks plus his Shoe Pak #8627 was repeated.

#7758
(1974)

Argyle that was reminiscent of Roller Skate Date #1405. The one-piece knit top looked like a gold turtleneck topped by an argyle vest. Argyle socks and brown slacks with elastic in back of the waist completed the set. $65.00

#7759
(1974)

Ken doll combined a big plaid flannel shirt with burgundy slacks with cargo pockets. A brown vinyl belt was included. $65.00

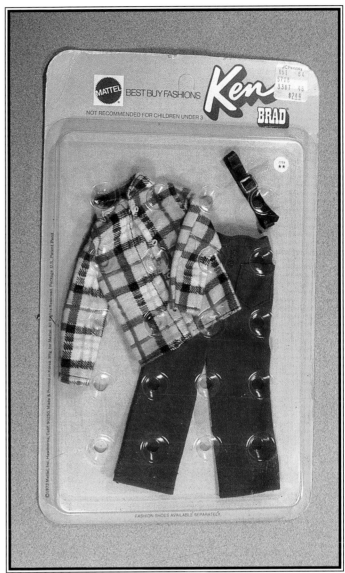

#7760
(1974)

This great vacation outfit featured the Hawaiian print that paired with the girls' outfits from this year. His bright shirt could pair with matching shorts or green slacks. He had a white sun visor to keep him cool. $65.00

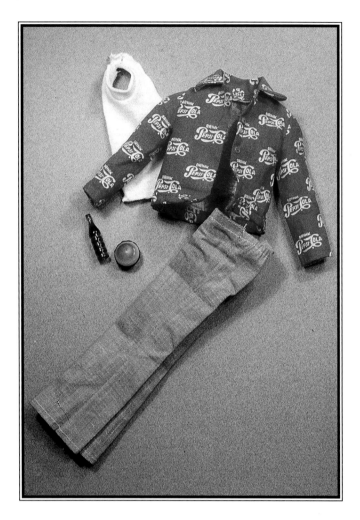

#7761
(1974)

Ken doll's Pepsi print outfit coordinated with the other dolls' Pepsi outfits. His Pepsi print shirt topped a white knit dickie and pale denim slacks. He had a plastic hamburger and a drink bottle. $95.00

#7762
(1974)

Ken doll's red suit had white stitching and buttons on both the jacket and pants. $65.00

#7763
(1974)

Ken doll's suit featured a red plaid jacket with blue velveteen lapels and pocket flaps. He had matching elastic back blue slacks and a white tricot dickie. $75.00

Ken Doll's Get-Ups 'n Go Fashions 1974

Ken doll's Camping Set # 7706 and Pilot #7707 were repeated. He had three new sets in 1974.

Bridegroom (1974 – 1975)
#7836

Ken doll looked handsome in his mid '70s tux look! He escorted Barbie doll down the aisle in a blue, floral brocade jacket with black velvet details and flower on his lapel. This brocade was the same fabric found in Barbie doll's #7840 Party Dress. He had a thin blue nylon ruffled front dickie with attached black velvet bow tie, black elastic back slacks, socks, and shoes. $100.00

Tennis (1974 – 1975)
#7837

Ken doll's tennis outfit matched Barbie doll's Get-Ups 'n Go outfit #7842 Tennis. He wore white shorts with a matching red/white/blue sweater set. He had a white fabric sun visor with clear bill, white knit socks and tennis shoes, a gray tennis racquet with red cover and white Mattel "M", and a yellow tennis ball. $75.00

Suit (1974)
#7838

Ken doll's business suit of the year was brown fleece with a white, tan, and brown pin stripe shirt and wide orange tie. He coordinated tan tricot socks and brown shoes to complete the set. $75.00

Sears Exclusive (1974)

The set contained three outfits: a blue chambray jacket and pants stitched in red; red plaid pants and shirt/sweater one-piece top with bow tie; argyle pants and orange knit shirt with argyle collar. $125.00

Skipper Doll's Looks for 1974

Bendable Skipper Doll (Germany) (1974)
#00-8126

Skipper doll, at right, had a unique two-piece swimsuit in royal blue. She is pictured with two Barbie dolls in swimsuits also available in Germany but not priced here. Skipper's suit only, $75.00

Skipper Doll's Best Buy Fashions 1974

Skipper doll's Shoe Pak #8624 was repeated this year.

#7770
(1974)

Skipper doll's Pepsi print wide leg pants were paired with a cute white crop top with double red ruffles. She had a hamburger and a drink bottle as accessories. This outfit coordinated with all other dolls' Pepsi Best Buy Fashions. $95.00

#7771
(1974)

The Hawaiian print worked well as a summer dress with pink ruffles. Skipper doll had matching panties to complete her look. This outfit coordinated with Barbie and Ken dolls' outfits with the same Hawaiian print. $50.00

#7773 (above)
(1974)

This cute dress coordinated with Barbie and Francie dolls' Best Buy Fashions. The white blouse look of the dress had two red shank buttons and a red vest look with the print skirt. A white slip with ruffle trim completed the look. $50.00

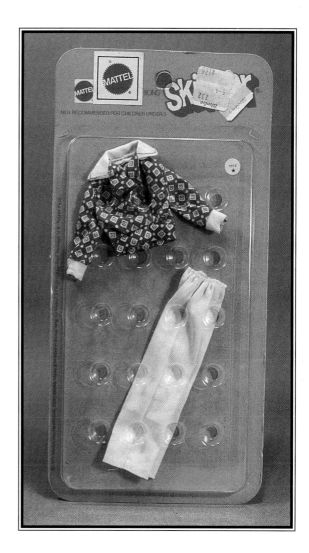

#7772 (above)
(1974)

Skipper doll's banded bottom print top with white collar and cuffs coordinated with Barbie doll's two-piece dress #7750. Two blue shank buttons accented the cuffs. Skipper doll had white pants and flats to complete her look. $50.00

#7774 (left)
(1974)

This cute long dress looked great with Barbie and Francie dolls' outfits fashioned from the same red calico. Skipper doll's featured a white blouse under the print jumper. A red bow at the neck and lace trim added nice detailing to the blouse. $50.00

#7775
(1974)

Skipper doll's granny dress had a yoke framed by a self ruffle. Ruffles trimmed the cuffs and hem as well. Contrasting black ribbon added more interest to the dress at the waist and sleeves. $50.00

Skipper Doll's Get-Ups 'n Go Outfits 1974

Two of Skipper doll's three 1973 Get-Ups 'n Go outfits were repeated. These were #7713 Sleep Set and #7714 Ballerina. She had two new sets in 1974.

#7848
(1974 – 1975)

Lots of beach accessories in bright colors were the highlights of this set. Skipper doll's red two-piece swimsuit contrasted her orange snorkel and face mask. She also had a long, colorful skirt, red and yellow halter, white shorts, print long dress with a yellow tricot top, print pants, and headband. She had a yellow terry beach towel, too. There were so many play possibilities! $75.00

#7847
(1974 – 1976)

This outfit coordinated with Barbie and Ken dolls' Bride and Groom Get-Ups 'n Go outfits. Skipper doll looked lovely in her yellow nylon dress with dots and white dotted sleeves. A ribbon with flower accented the waist. A white textured nylon pinafore added more interest. She had a yellow tulle headband hat with three white flowers, a bouquet of pink and white flowers on a yellow tulle back with a cord tie instead of ribbon, and white flats. $100.00

Sears Exclusive
1974

Skipper doll's fashion pak from Sears featured blue chambray jacket; mini skirt and shorts; a red with white dots tricot crop top with ruffle; white tricot knee socks; a floral dress with ribbon accent at the empire waistline; and two pairs of shoes, pink and white. Also include were pink tights; leotard; and a tan faux fur coat with brown vinyl trim at the neck that fastened with two large goldtone bead buttons. $125.00

Francie Doll's Ensembles for 1974

Francie Doll's Best Buy Fashions 1974

Francie doll's Shoe Pak #8625 was repeated this year and she had six new Best Buy Fashions and two new Get-Ups 'n Go outfits as well as two repeated ones.

#7764
(1974)

This pink jumper had suspenders that fastened with hooks and bead buttons. The jumper and floral blouse coordinated with #7765. $65.00

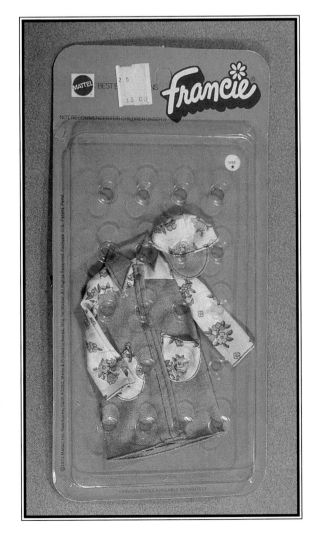

#7765
(1974)

This set coordinated with Francie doll's other Best Buy outfit #7764. This cute pink and print coat had a matching cap. $65.00

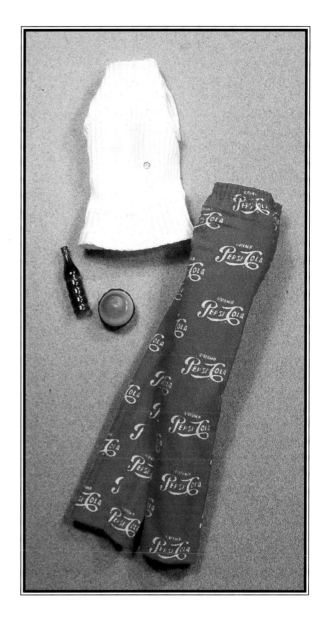

#7766
(1974)

Francie doll joined the Pepsi generation in her white, poor boy top that came in smooth or ribbed knit fabric over Pepsi print slacks. She had a plastic hamburger and a drink bottle as accessories. $95.00

#7767
(1974)

Francie doll looked lovely in her flocked dot evening ensemble. The full skirt featured twin ruffles with black edging and a black bodice. Her dotted shawl featured the ruffle treatment and she had a two contrasting flowers at the waist, one red, one purple, with a fuchsia bow. $95.00

#7768
(1974)

Francie doll's calico sundress coordinated with Barbie and Skipper dolls' calico looks. The puckered bodice had a short skirt with ruffle at the hem. Red ribbon formed the straps and also the hat band for her contrasting yellow hat. $50.00

#7769
(1974)

This pretty granny dress looked great with Barbie and Skipper dolls' calico prints. Francie doll's dress had eyelet flutter sleeves and bodice inset. A wide yellow satin ribbon accented her waist. $50.00

Francie Doll's Get-Ups 'n Go Outfits 1974

Two of Francie doll's three Get-Ups 'n Go outfits from 1973 were continued. These were #7710 Beach and #7711 Cheerleader. She also had two new ones in 1974.

#7845
(1974 – 1975)

Francie doll did great figure 8's when she wore her cute, red flannel skating dress and jacket trimmed in white fun fur. Her mittens were red with furry tops and she had a fun fur bonnet that tied with a red ribbon, red jersey tights, and white ice skates. $75.00

#7846
(1974 – 1975)

Francie doll could go camping with the gang now that she had her own floral and solid peach flannel sleeping bag! She wore cute shorts in blue stripes with matching jacket and white vinyl belt. Red stitching, buttons, red tricot knee socks and halter, plus flannel and brown vinyl backpack added interest to the look. She wore brown hiking boots (these were Barbie doll's skates molded in brown plastic without any wheels or blades for skates). $65.00

Tutti And Chris Dolls From Europe In 1974

The dolls in their original outfits, and outfits sold separately were not on the market in the United States. Twelve outfits for Tutti and Chris dolls were shown in the 1974 German booklet.

Tutti Doll
Original Outfit #8128
(1974)

She wore her original dress with print top and blue floral skirt with turquoise bow at the waist. She wore white bow shoes and had a pale pink comb and brush. The ribbon in her hair was pink. Complete, $175.00

Chris Doll
Original Outfit #8130
(1974)

The cute doll wore a floral print dress with pink panties and white bow shoes. She had a pale pink comb and brush as well as her tiny brass barrette. Complete, $175.00

The twelve ensembles from 1974:

#7980 Mein neuer Mantel $75.00
#7981 Ich geh schlafen $75.00
#7982 Hosenanzug $75.00
#7983 Kinderparty $75.00 (not shown)
#8502 Bequem and praktisch $75.00
#8503 Grobe Reise $75.00
#8504 Schnee flockchen $75.00
#8505 Eingeladen zum Geburtstag $75.00
#8591 Ich geh spazieren $75.00
#8592 Blue jeans und Ringelpulli $75.00
#8593 Ich geh spielen $75.00
#8594 Regentropfen $75.00

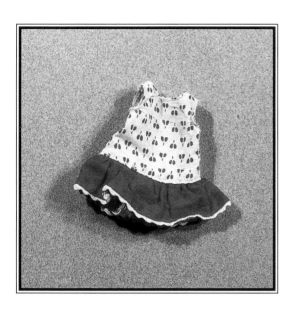

TUTTI®-Kleider

Kleider für TUTTI® und CHRIS®

00-8505 Eingeladen
zum Geburtstag

00-8502
Bequem und

00-8503
Große
Reise

00-8504
Schnee-
flöckchen

Todd Doll from Europe in 1974

There were four outfits shown for Todd doll in the 1974 Mattel Germany booklet as well as Todd doll in his original outfit.

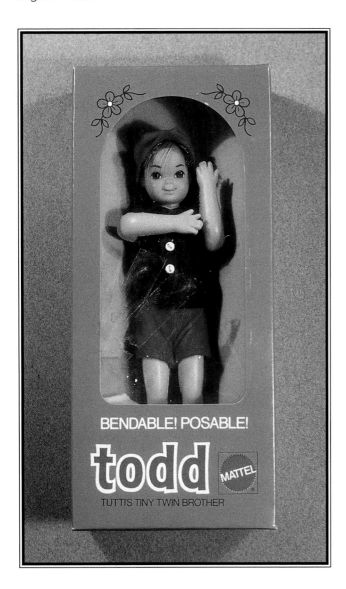

Todd Doll
Original Outfit (1974)
#8129

The adorable doll was dressed in a red cap and shorts with navy shirt with white buttons. White tricot socks and white strange looking shoes that are too long for Todd doll were included. The doll with striped navy and white shorts (right) was from Switzerland. Complete, $175.00

Todd Doll's Outfits for 1974

#7984 Jeans-Auzug $75.00
#7985 Ausflug $75.00
#7986 Hubschangezogen $75.00
#7987 Sport-Fan $75.00

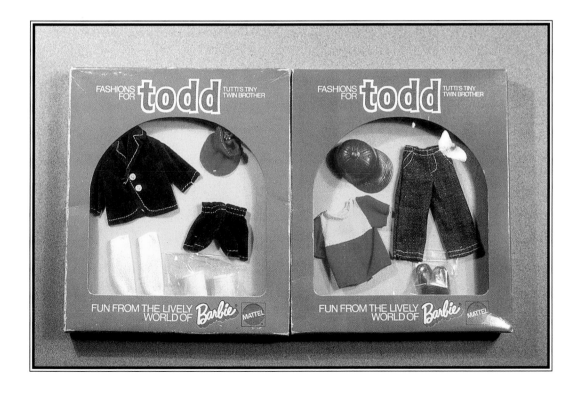

Schroeder's
ANTIQUES
Price Guide

. . . is the #1 best-selling antiques & collectibles value guide on the market today, and here's why . . .

• More than 300 advisors, well-known dealers, and top-notch collectors work together with our editors to bring you accurate information regarding pricing and identification.

• More than 45,000 items in almost 500 categories are listed along with hundreds of sharp original photos that illustrate not only the rare and unusual, but the common, popular collectibles as well.

• Each large close-up shot shows important details clearly. Every subject is represented with histories and background information, a feature not found in any of our competitors' publications.

• Our editors keep abreast of newly developing trends, often adding several new categories a year as the need arises.

If it merits the interest of today's collector, you'll find it in *Schroeder's*. And you can feel confident that the information we publish is up to date and accurate. Our advisors thoroughly check each category to spot inconsistencies, listings that may not be entirely reflective of market dealings, and lines too vague to be of merit. Only the best of the lot remains for publication.

Without doubt, you'll find
SCHROEDER'S ANTIQUES PRICE GUIDE
the only one to buy for
reliable information and values.

COLLECTOR BOOKS
A Division of Schroeder Publishing Co., Inc.